DECEMBER 1917

RE-VISITING THE HALIFAX EXPLOSION

JANET KITZ & JOAN PAYZANT

NIMBUS PUBLISHING

Nimbus Publishing Limited
PO Box 9166
Halifax, NS B3K 5M8
(902) 455-4286

Printed and bound in Canada

Interior design: Margaret Issenman, MGDC
Front cover: Min Landry, Wink Design

Library and Archives Canada Cataloguing in Publication

Kitz, Janet F., 1930-
December 1917 : re-visiting the Halifax explosion / Janet Kitz and Joan Payzant.

Includes bibliographical references and index.
ISBN 1-55109-566-1

1. Halifax Explosion, Halifax, N.S., 1917. I. Payzant, Joan M. II. Title.

FC2346.4.K577 2006 971.6'22503 C2006-905496-7

We acknowledge the financial support of the Government of Canada through the Book Publishing Industry Development Program (BPIDP) and the Canada Council, and of the Province of Nova Scotia through the Department of Tourism, Culture and Heritage for our publishing activities.

The Canada Council for the Arts | Le Conseil des Arts du Canada

Contents

Acknowledgements

Garry Shutlak was responsible for most of the material on Mulgrave Park, North Street Station, and much of the north end of Dartmouth and Tufts Cove. He also added the markers to the main maps. He has been a rich source of information concerning buildings, streets, and much more.

Gary Castle photographed modern scenes and buildings and reproduced many old photographs for the section on Halifax. Without his skill and unfailing willingness to spend time and effort on the project, this book would not have been possible. Matthew Hughson, with a keen eye for the best light and angle, photographed modern-day Dartmouth sites in colour.

Jim Simpson's guided North End walks showed his detailed knowledge of the area, and he has also been very helpful about individual houses and other details on both sides of the harbour.

The authors also wish to acknowledge the following individuals for their assistance: Edith (Orr) Clattenburg; Charles Vaughn; Sister Stanislaus; Blair Beed; Francoise Longhurst; the Fairview Cemetery authorities; Marilyn Gurney, of the Maritime Command Museum; Anita Price and Lisa O'Neill of the Dartmouth Heritage Museum; Harold Merklinger; Patricia Sutherland of the Halifax North Memorial Library; Dan Conlin of the Maritime Museum of the Atlantic; the staff of Nova Scotia Archives and Records Management.

Finally, the following people provided interviews that were invaluable resources: Wallace Baker; Donald Barteaux; Mollie (Kuhn) Campbell; Margaret (Kuhn) Campbell; Dr. W. Creighton; Dorothy (Swetnam) Hare; Isabel (Grey) Horne; Walter Murphy; Jean (Crowdis) Murray; James Pattison; Millicent (Upham) Swindells; Barbara (Orr) Thompson; Archie Upham; Annie (Liggins) Welsh

Introduction

HALIFAX AND DARTMOUTH: A BRIEF HISTORY

The catastrophic explosion of December 6, 1917, is one of the most important events in the history of Halifax and Dartmouth. It caused devastating losses and permanently altered the landscape of the two cities. Much of nineteenth-century Halifax and Dartmouth was swept away on that terrible day, and many distinctive features of the contemporary landscape came into being through the reconstruction. To understand the origins of the explosion, however, one must look to the two cities' history, and especially to their naval and marine heritage.

The European settlement of Halifax began in June 1749, when the British HMS *Sphinx* arrived off what is now Point Pleasant Park. One by one, thirteen transport ships approached to drop anchor near the warship that had been their escort. They held some 2,500 eager settlers, lured by promises of a fine new life in the place then known as Chebucto. What they saw was a vast forest divided by inlets of the sea. When clearing the shoreline facing the Atlantic proved difficult, and the site proved too exposed to bad weather, the settlers re-boarded their ships, and, with increasing awe, sailed into one of the finest harbours in the world. There they founded a town that Edward Cornwallis, leader of the expedition, named Halifax, to honour Lord Halifax, president of the Board of Trade, which was responsible for the colonization of Nova Scotia.

The original purpose of having a settlement on the east coast of the colony of Nova Scotia was to counter the French fortress of Louisbourg in Cape Breton. The Board of Trade had offered fifty acres of land to every qualified settler, plus ten extra acres for every member of his family, as well as arms, ammunition, and supplies necessary for their successful beginnings in a new land. There were added bonuses to tempt military personnel. Officers received land grants in accordance with their rank, those above the rank of captain being offered six hundred acres, plus thirty acres for each member of their family. Everyone was to have rations for one year. There were promises of civil liberty and proper defence against attack, whether by the native people or the French. It sounded almost too good to be true. In order to attract people with better skills for creating a new settlement than might be expected from men trained to fight, the same terms were extended to "carpenters, shipwrights, smiths, masons, joiners, brickmakers, bricklayers and all other artificers necessary in building or husbandry."

Unfortunately, the majority of prospective settlers who arrived in the first wave had few of the required skills. Many were Londoners; few were farmers, fishermen, or builders. The new governor, Lord Cornwallis, wrote to London, complaining that only one hundred soldiers and some two hundred tradesmen had arrived. Attempts to establish a new town were fraught with difficulty. A small number of foreign Protestants, mainly German and Swiss, provided the most useful skills.

Stories of drunkenness and rowdy behaviour forced the British authorities to make great efforts to find more suitable settlers. In the second wave of settlers, arriving between 1750 and 1752, came some 2,500 foreign Protestants, nearly doubling the population. Many were resettled in what became Lunenburg in 1753, but sufficient numbers remained in Halifax, where they were largely responsible for the building of fortifications and dwelling houses. Most of the foreign Protestants lived in the northern section of

Halifax from Georges Island, 1880

the city, and it was there that the Little Dutch Church, a faulty translation of "Deutsch," meaning German, was created. They are also remembered in street names, such as Gottingen Street, Gerrish Street, Merkel Street, and Brunswick Street.

Because of its strategic position, the British government had chosen the location of Halifax to provide a naval and military base in North America. Not surprisingly, the city has had a strong military presence ever since, and the harbour has sheltered some of the largest fleets that ever crossed the Atlantic. After war with France broke out in 1756, the need for better defences became more urgent. Forts were built or strengthened, and in 1759 an Order-in-Council established the King's Yard, which contained facilities for anchorage and the repair of naval ships. These Imperial army and naval bases took part in all the wars of the British Empire. By 1790, the Dockyard stretched along the harbour from Gerrish Street as far as Young Street. Gradually, Halifax grew from a military outpost to a bustling commercial town, whose prosperity increased during times of war.

Halifax was incorporated as a city in 1841, by which point its population had reached approximately fifteen thousand. Ships packed with large numbers of Irish immigrants, forced from their country by hardship and famine, had arrived in the intervening years. With every threat of attack the garrison of troops was strengthened. After discharge from the army, it was common for soldiers, many Scots or Irish, to remain in the town with their families. New arrivals from the American colonies to the south, usually fishermen and traders, also increased the population.

Over the course of the nineteenth century, the development of ground transportation began to change the shape of the city. By the late 1850s a railway line had been built, reaching a depot of wooden buildings at the foot of Duffus Street, named the Richmond Yards.

It linked the port of Halifax to the inland crops and produce, encouraging export and increasing prosperity. The new, grand North Street Station, opened by Prime Minister Alexander Mackenzie in 1877, became the main passenger depot. With its great glass dome and luxurious fittings, it was described as one of the finest railway stations in the whole country. With the railway and the construction of Campbell Road, which followed the perimeter of the Dockyard, the possibility of development increased in the northern part of the peninsula, beyond the original town site. Sir Colin Campbell, a former army officer and lieutenant-governor of Nova Scotia from 1834 till 1840, envisaged a road that would follow the whole perimeter of the settlement. Campbell Road, completed while he was in office, was the section that ran as far as the north end of the Dockyard, enabling the area later called Richmond, but originally intended to be named Campbelltown, to be settled.

The building of roads and railways had attracted thousands of labourers. They needed places to live. Family homes and large boarding houses appeared. Industries attracted by rail and sea transport followed. The settlement grew and developed, acquiring the name Richmond from the Richmond Yards, which were probably named for Richmond, Virginia, source of raw materials unloaded at the yards. Churches, schools, stores, parkland, and all the other requirements of a community had soon taken over the former farmland. Row housing was mainly along the harbour. The rest of Richmond appeared almost rural, with parks (like Fort Needham and Mulgrave Park), gardens, barns, room for various animals, and large houses, built by factory owners, managers, doctors, and other professionals, all of whom preferred to live in the place where they worked. The Graving Dock, Hillis and Sons' Refinery, the Acadia Sugar Refinery, Gunn's

Richmond Station, nd

Flour Mills, and the Richmond Printing Company were among the leading employers, but the railway, the Dockyard, and their subsidiaries were the mainstay.

By 1917 Halifax was a bustling city of more than fifty thousand people. The early years of the twentieth century had been characterized by progressive reform efforts, which had gone a long way towards modernizing the city. Infrastructure was improved, new recreational and voluntary associations emerged, and education received unprecedented attention. Likewise, the city's cultural life was being altered by new forms of leisure and entertainment. A glimpse of that cultural life can be found in the 1916 city directory, which listed the city's "Amusement Places." These included the Academy of Music on Pleasant Street, Acker's Vaudeville Theatre on Sackville Street, the Casino Theatre on Gottingen Street, the Empire Theatre on Jacob Street, the Halifax Arena Co. Ltd. on Louisburg Street, the Halifax Shooting Gallery on Upper Water Street, the King Edward Theatre on Barrington Street, Melville Park on the west side of the Northwest Arm, the Orpheus Theatre on Granville Street, and the Strand Theatre on Sackville Street.

The listings in the *Evening Mail* for Friday, November 30, 1917, reveal more of the colourful varieties of entertainment available in Halifax. The Orpheus Theatre was showing *The Hostage*, a tale of love or duty, with a two-reel comedy, *The Hero*, as an extra. The Casino, on Monday, Tuesday, and Wednesday, offered *For The Freedom Of The World*, "a stupendous war theme." The Empire, which also boasted a new heating system, was showing *Redemption*, with Evelyn Thaw and her son, Russell Thaw. Her name was very well known because of a notorious 1910 murder case, in which her husband had murdered her former lover. The Academy of Music, meanwhile, announced "a play that is a novelty," *Which One Shall I Marry?* The Strand, described as "Refined Vaudeville," had a varied programme that was very much a product of its time, consisting of a pair of "Polite Conversationalists and Vocalists," "Black Face Comedians in Mirth and Music," a gentleman who performed whistling imitations, a singing and dancing novelty, a woman whose specialty was "Novelty in Acrobatics," and the fourth chapter of a serial, designed to ensure regular attendance, *The Grey Ghost*.

Dining out was always popular in Halifax, so it is not surprising to find fifty-eight restaurants listed in the city directory, including a lunch wagon on Barrington Street, the

Church of England Coffee Rooms on Upper Water Street, the Khaki Club for Army and Navy on Granville Street, the Oriental Star Café on Duke Street, and others of different kinds. Ice cream dealers and confectioners were also fairly abundant. In wartime, bars and liquor stores were not supposed to sell alcohol, and "blind pigs," as they were known, sprang up to fill the void.

For more intellectual pursuits, the city boasted seven lending libraries: the Cambridge Library at Royal Artillery Park, the Citizens' Free Library at City Hall, Arthur Cleveland's Lending Library on Gottingen Street, Connolly's Modern Lending Library and Davidson's Popular Lending Library on Barrington Street, the Legislative Library in the Province Building, and the Provincial Science Library at the Technical College on Spring Garden Road. Some were used mainly for reference, but the private libraries lent books of various types, usually on a subscription basis.

Boating clubs, mainly on the Northwest Arm, provided opportunities for both sailing and rowing. There were two curling rinks, on South Bland Street and Agricola Street. There were also two skating rinks, on Louisburg Street and South Street. Thirty-eight music teachers, mainly of piano, but some for violin, offered their services. The Philharmonic Orchestra on Victoria Road and the Taylor Concert Company on Shirley Street catered to music lovers.

The business life of Halifax was also bustling and varied. Chinese laundries numbered thirty-seven, presumably catering to those who wanted to have their tablecloths or shirts

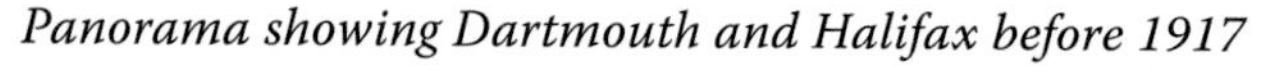
Panorama showing Dartmouth and Halifax before 1917

properly starched, as well as handling large items like bed clothes before automatic washers and dryers came into use. There were numerous milliners, necessary when hats were still often handmade. Dressmakers and tailors abounded, as ready-made clothing was not as plentiful as it is today. Services that we no longer expect were four umbrella repairers and two taxidermists. Twenty-two newspapers, not all daily, twenty steamship lines, two tourist services, and twenty-four second-hand goods stores were in existence.

In spite of some signs of modernity, the culture of Halifax was still strongly colonial, and traditional fraternal societies, organized by nationality, remained important. Prominent among these were the North British Society, which had been founded as the Scottish Guild of Merchants in 1763; the Charitable Irish Society, founded 1786; and the Royal St. George Society, founded by English colonists in 1786. All were created to help new immigrants, and still exist today largely as social clubs.

Masonic lodges were also established early in the history of Halifax. Some artisan settlers were members before leaving their native countries. Over the centuries, these lodges grew and became an important part of Halifax society. Parades and festivities during the Natal Day festival have always reflected the culture of Halifax, with national costumes, and bands playing the music of different countries, as well as military and naval contingents.

The churches, which had always been prominent in Halifax society, continued to supply most of the social life for their parishioners, with meetings, socials, choirs with frequent practices, teas, educational talks, and all kinds of get-togethers.

Across the harbour from Halifax, Dartmouth was still very much a small town in 1917, although it had been incorporated as early as 1873. The population stood at around 6,500.

New development was gradually spreading out to its borders, but downtown Portland Street was the heart of the town, lined with stores of every kind, a gathering centre for weekend shopping and neighbourly sociability. Even if people did not know each other by name, they probably knew each other by sight as they met on a Friday or Saturday night. This close-knit feeling within the town reached its peak on the first Wednesday of each August, when Dartmouth's Natal Day was celebrated with flair and excitement. Ships' horns, the town fire bell, and other noisemakers started the day at eight o'clock in the morning. Then came road races, a parade that the whole town turned out to watch, ball games on the commons, a regatta on Lake Banook, and a spectacular fireworks display over the lake. Alas, though, Natal Day was not held during the First World War, because the community was thrown into patriotic activity to assist the war effort.

Dartmouth came into existence in 1750, one year after the founding of Halifax, when more English settlers arrived in the harbour on the ship *Alderney.* They were sent to the opposite shore of the harbour and became the first citizens of a new village, Dartmouth, named for Dartmouth in England. It was slow to expand and prosper because of raids by the Mi'kmaq, who, not unnaturally, were affronted by the takeover of their own village sites.

In fact, had it not been for the American Revolution, Dartmouth might have disappeared altogether, as family after family moved away to more congenial sites. Life was

The harbour in 2005

breathed back into the settlement by Quaker Whalers, who were given grants of land in Dartmouth by Governor Parr with plans to move their whaling business there from Nantucket. Samuel Starbuck came in 1785 with a group to prepare the site for the wharves and whaling factory, and the following year his partner and friend Timothy Folger came with a second contingent, bringing families and supplies. Very quickly, the town came to life, with new houses, wharves, and buildings establishing the whaling business in Dartmouth Cove. Land was cleared to make the Dartmouth Common, where cattle could graze. A new Quaker meeting house served as both church and school. For a few years Dartmouth was busy and prosperous. Other Loyalists arrived too, many from the Sandemanian sect in Massachusetts, settling mostly in what is today the Woodlawn/Westphal area. Unfortunately, almost as suddenly as they had come, the British government exerted political pressure to move the Quakers and their whaling industry to Milford Haven in Wales. A few of the Quakers remained in Dartmouth maintaining their quality of good citizenship, as well as the physical presence of wharves, houses, and the Dartmouth Common. Only a fraction of this land remains today.

At this time, prominent men in Halifax dreamt of a waterway to cross the province from Halifax Harbour to the Bay of Fundy, through lakes, rivers, and man-made canals. As their dreams evolved, surveyors, architects, and then stonemasons from Ireland and Scotland came to Dartmouth. The resulting Shubenacadie Canal was not a success, but some of the families stayed. Gradually other businesses were founded, and life became more stable in Dartmouth. Shipbuilders and sailmakers set up their businesses on the waterfront. Two privately owned ferry services started at the north

The Dartmouth Ferry Terminal, c.1915

and south ends of the village, using large rowboats. With the invention of steam engines, the Halifax Steamboat Company put three paddle-wheeled steam ferries on the ferry route. Two or three grist mills, a tannery, and a small nail factory hired workers. In the mid-1800s Dartmouth joined the Industrial Revolution, with several industries employing large workforces: Starr Manufactory, Consumers' Cordage, the Halifax Brewery, and Mott's Chocolate Factory. A few years later, the Acadia Sugar Refinery began production. Then, with the fast growth of the car and truck industry, Imperial Oil opened its refinery just south of the sugar refinery.

Because of its lakes and hills Dartmouth has always been a grand place for both summer and winter sports activities. In the early twentieth century, St. George's Tennis Club,

Starr Manufacturing

Brightwood Golf Club, Banook Canoe Club, and the North Star Rowing Club were popular spots in the summer. In the winter, empty lots with hills, lakes, and ponds provided opportunity for coasting and skating. After a big snowstorm, the steep streets were exciting for double runners and toboggans—these were the days before snow-ploughs. Dartmouth had a magnificent rink perched on top of Synnott's hill at the corner of Windmill Road and Wyse Road. Even the Halifax Skating Club was lured over by the promise of free ferry tickets and the wonderful music of a Dartmouth band, the Harpers.

In those days before radios and movie theatres were common, churches provided much of the social life for their congregations with gatherings for different age groups—Brownies and Cubs, Scouts and Guides, Canadian Girls in Training (CGIT), and Tuxis for younger members. Groups for young people and for older men and women organized concerts, potluck suppers, and other entertainments to help long winter evenings pass pleasantly.

HALIFAX, DARTMOUTH, AND THE FIRST WORLD WAR

With the start of war in 1914, life suddenly took on a more serious aspect in both Halifax and Dartmouth. Although Canada was by then a self-governing colony, it was nevertheless committed by the British government's declaration of war on Germany on August 4. The first years cost Canada tens of thousands of military casualties. Among these casualties were significant numbers of Haligonians and Dartmouthians, whose names are recorded on the two cities' war memorials.

As had happened throughout the town's history, war brought prosperity and activity to Halifax. Every fort in the area was soon fully staffed for the defence of the city and harbour. Troops were being trained for overseas duty in various large military spaces, such as McNabs Island, York Redoubt, Wellington Barracks, and the Armouries. The streets were alive day and night with troops, workers coming and going from different shifts, people moving with a sense of urgency. Sailors added to the crowds in the streets, most in naval uniform, and the merchant seamen in a variety of garbs. Only allied sailors were allowed ashore. The neutrals had to remain on board ship. There might have been spies among them.

The war also meant the return of the British navy after an absence of almost a decade. In March 1905 the British Royal Navy had transferred its headquarters to Bermuda. In 1907 the Dockyard had become the property of the Canadian government with the proviso that, if necessary in time of war, the facilities would be made available to British forces. It took three years for the Royal Canadian Navy to be established and for the yard to come into use again.

In 1910 HMCS *Niobe* and HMCS *Rainbow* were purchased from Britain to form the nucleus of the Royal Canadian Navy. By 1917 *Niobe* had been permanently moored at the dockyard, and, with various wooden structures added on its decks, served as the offices of the Chief Commanding Officer for Naval Intelligence, and for naval training.

Throughout the war, merchant ships gathered in the Bedford Basin and crossed the dangerous waters of the Atlantic under escort of heavily armed warships. The harbour saw ships of many kinds. Passenger ships were common, now carrying huge numbers of troops rather than pleasure seekers or immigrants. Cargo ships from all allied and neutral nations—to be loaded with food, grain from the prairies, horses and their fodder, all the supplies needed for war—lay at most docks. Hospital ships arrived with

HMT Olympic, *with dazzle paint to confuse enemy gunners*

the seriously wounded, those who had lost limbs or sight. Military hospitals soon became overcrowded, with a new facility being built at Camp Hill. Unfortunately, the city was better equipped for military and naval casualties than for civilian medical problems.

German attack was always a fear, and submarines were spotted not too far from shore. Few lights showed at night, as a blackout system was enforced. Two anti-submarine nets stretched across the harbour, with gates in them that were opened at different times of day but never at night. By early 1917, so many ships had been lost to enemy action that a convoy system was put in place. The Canadian navy itself had not yet been completely organized when the war began, so it originally concentrated on east coast patrols. There were few naval ships, but trawlers and drifters were quickly converted, and motor launches were useful for special duties.

Halifax's factories, now involved in war work, required extra employees. Soon, every boarding house in Richmond was filled with workers from different parts of Canada and even Europe. One became home to a group of young Scottish women who came to work at Davie's Sack Manufacturers on East Young Street, locally known as the Bag Factory. The uses for sacks had multiplied with the increased exports to Europe.

Halifax dockyard in 1907

Dartmouth was also touched by the war. A large number of Dartmouth men and boys enlisted and by 1917 were serving overseas or in the new Canadian navy. Over a dozen Dartmouth women went overseas as well, serving as nursing sisters. Citizens remaining at home did their part to help with the war effort. Fairs were held on the Common or in the rink to raise money for Belgian relief; two newly formed IODE chapters sent Christmas parcels to boys overseas, enclosing hand-knit socks, mitts, and hats for them. A Red Cross chapter was formed to gather medical supplies and comforts. Concerts were held in St. Peter's Hall or in the theatre on King Street, with the proceeds going to help the war effort. A group of Dartmouth men volunteered to collect for the Canadian Patriotic Fund, which helped the families of servicemen, and they found generous support from local businesses and the town itself.

Anti-submarine nets stretched across the harbour.

A copy of a photo from a German newspaper, showing an enemy ship attacked by a submarine. The caption means "Sunk without trace."

All of this war-related activity involved the people of Halifax and Dartmouth, who realized that they were in danger from an enemy attack on the shipping in the harbour.

The situation in France was so desperate that agents were buying enormous quantities of munitions in the United States, enough to need forty to fifty ships every two weeks. Thus, munitions ships were no rare visitors to Halifax. Many of the British ships also carried munitions, but usually as only part of their load. Before the war, ships carrying dangerous cargo had not been allowed to enter the harbour, but had to remain at one of the outer quays. The war had eased those regulations, as the outer quays were too exposed to enemy submarines.

By December 1917 the outlook had become somewhat more optimistic. The huge losses of shipping had been greatly reduced. The United States had entered the war. Allied armies were advancing, retaking positions previously lost. Canadian soldiers distinguished themselves in the capture of Passchendaele in November. The feared telegrams still arrived, announcing that a son or husband had been killed or wounded, and black armbands were far from uncommon, but the desperate losses of the earlier years had lessened. Many families had relatives abroad; some had several, like Lieutenant-Governor Grant, whose five sons were all serving members of the forces. By the end of 1917, they were becoming more hopeful that they might be united again before too many more years had passed. Occasional home leave from the front was now being granted. It was even possible to look forward to Christmas, and a special fair was advertised at the Exhibition Grounds, on Windsor Street.

A convoy gathered in Bedford Basin. Richmond Yards are in the foreground.

DECEMBER 6, 1917

The events leading up to the explosion of December 6 had begun several days earlier. The neutral Norwegian ship *Imo*, captained by Haakon From, had lain in Bedford Basin for three days, en route from Holland to New York to pick up relief supplies for war-torn Belgium. The words "BELGIAN RELIEF" were clearly printed on its side to save it from submarine attack. As a neutral ship, it needed no convoy, but had been held up because fuel supplies arrived too late the night before, after the gates in the anti-submarine nets were closed. The captain and crew were eager to be on the move. Those three days in the Bedford Basin, unable to go ashore, had seemed endless.

SS Imo *after the explosion*

Meanwhile, the French *Mont Blanc*, captained by Aimé Le Medec, arrived from New York on the evening of December 5, fully loaded with munitions. The ship reported to the inspection boat, and was told that it was not possible to continue through the harbour, not because of the ship's cargo, but because the gates in the nets were closed. An experienced

SS Mont Blanc

local pilot, Charles Mackey, straight off another ship, boarded *Mont Blanc,* and the ship anchored off McNabs Island for the night. "We are all explosives," said Captain Le Medec. The stevedores in New York had worn cloth covers on their boots to prevent sparks. The crew was thankful to be in a safe harbour. On the voyage from New York, they had kept a constant lookout for enemy submarines. They hoped to be able to be part of an escorted convoy that would bring them across the ocean in relative safety. Actually, it was unlikely that *Mont Blanc* would be permitted to join the convoy in the basin. It was an old ship and too slow to keep up, thus endangering other ships. The ship's captain probably would have been given sealed orders by Naval Command, including a map of the safest route across the Atlantic.

At seven thirty on the morning of December 6, both ships left anchor. *Imo,* also with an experienced pilot, William Hayes, reported to the guard ship, and though it was given permission to proceed, it could not reach its proper channel, on the Halifax side—another ship was in the way. *Imo* was still on the Dartmouth side as it entered the Narrows, where a tugboat, *Stella Maris,* towing two scows, approached from the Halifax shore, forcing *Imo* to remain off course.

Mont Blanc steamed gently along its proper course, until, nearing the Narrows, the men on the bridge, with complete disbelief, saw a ship heading directly towards them. There

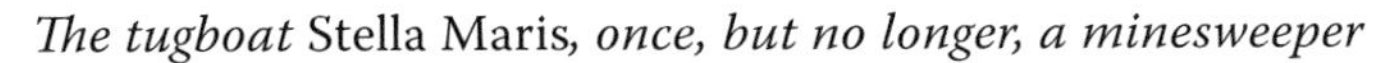

The tugboat Stella Maris, *once, but no longer, a minesweeper*

were whistle signals from both ships, as they tried to avoid each other. Misunderstandings, bad judgment, possibly some panic on *Mont Blanc* ensued. Then…collision! *Imo* struck *Mont Blanc*, not all that hard, but breaking through the metal prow and causing sparks.

It did not take long for the sparks to ignite the benzol, a highly inflammable type of gasoline, loaded on *Mont Blanc*'s decks, nor for the fire to spread. Expecting the ship to blow up immediately, the captain, pilot, and crew (forty men in all) clambered quickly into the two lifeboats and rowed with almost superhuman strength due to their panic, speedily covering the considerable distance to the Dartmouth shore.

Imo's Norwegian captain ordered his helmsman to head for more open water where the ship could turn and head back to the basin to assess its condition. Collisions were not unknown, but they rarely caused severe damage.

The fire on *Mont Blanc* became ever more spectacular as the ship drifted slowly towards the Richmond shore, the ammunition on board shooting up through the great cloud of smoke, flashing and sparking.

To those on that shore, it seemed almost like an entertainment with fireworks. No one recognized the danger. Work in the factories stopped, as the windows were crammed

A map of the harbour, showing the location of the explosion

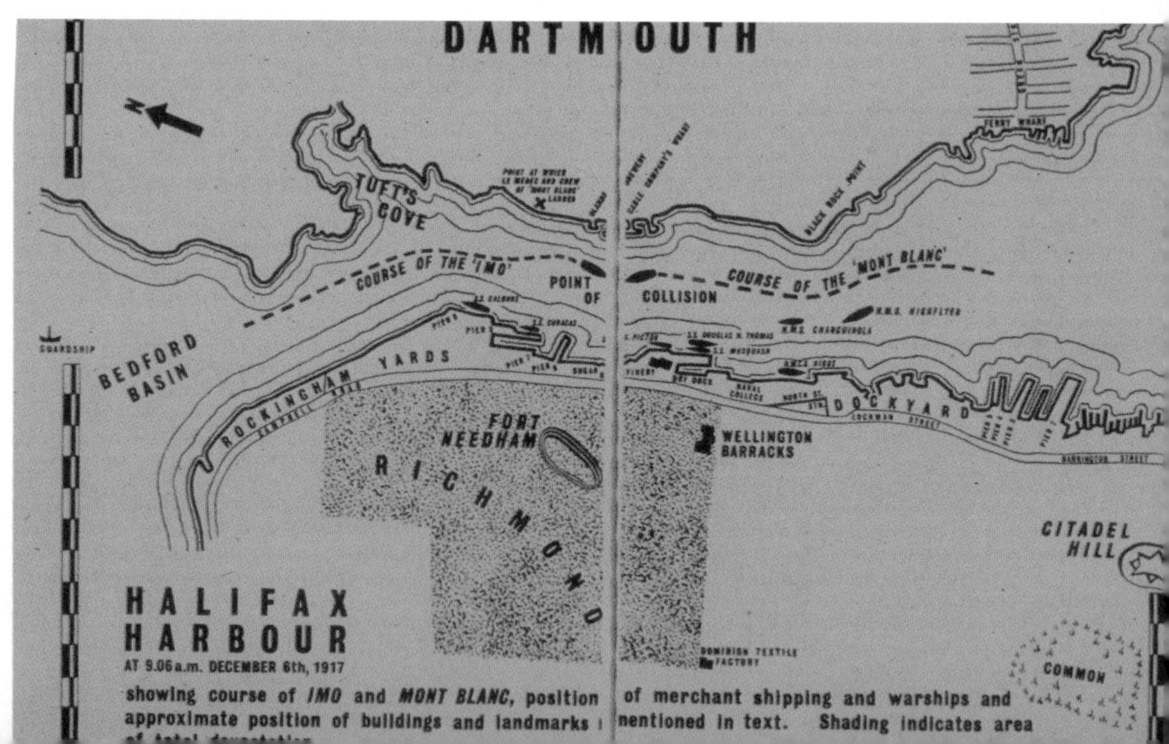

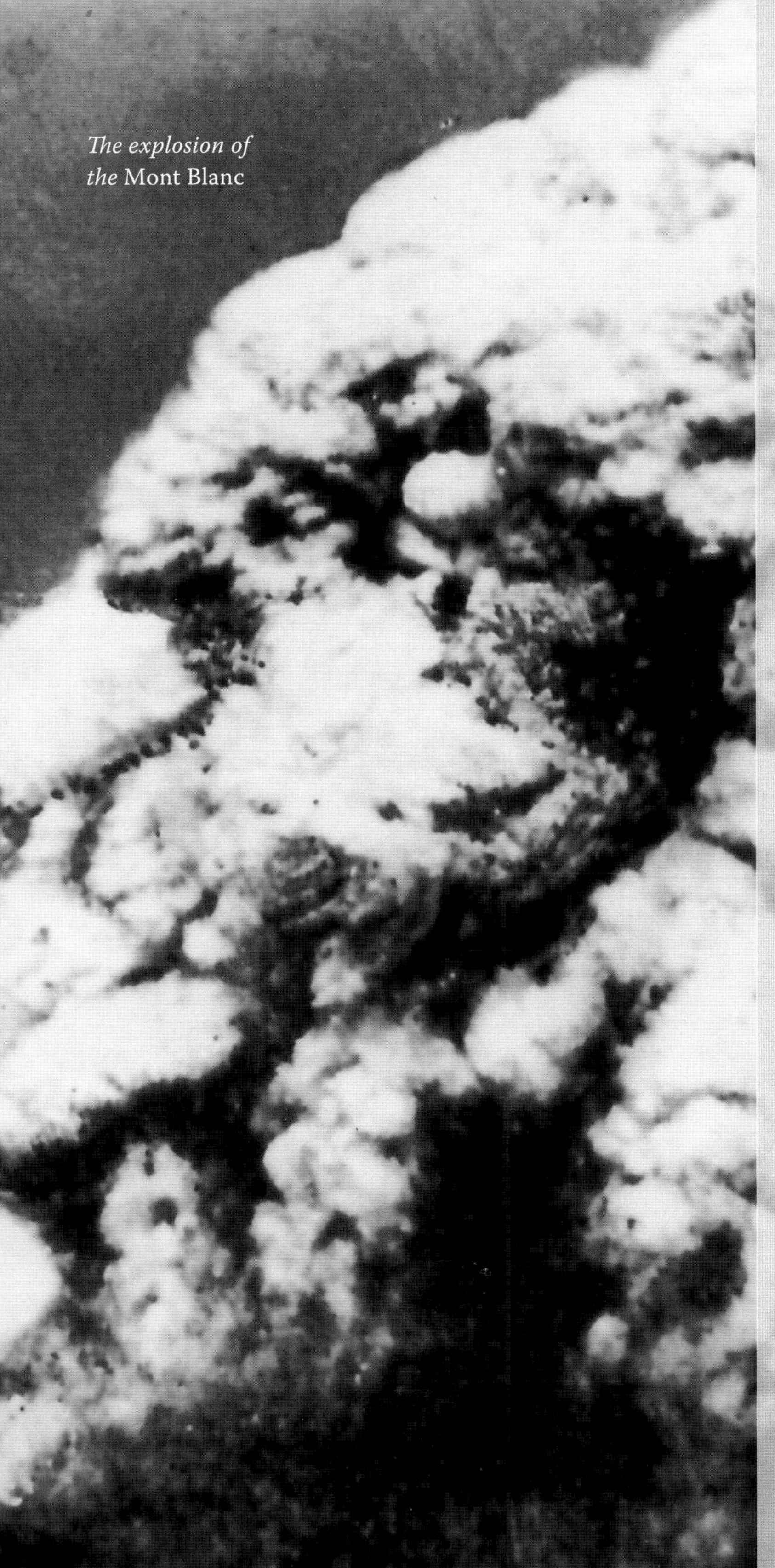
The explosion of the Mont Blanc

All French newspapers reported the disaster at Richmond, the news coming from either Montreal or New York. The first reports, on December 7, were inaccurate, attributing the explosion to the blowing up of an arsenal, with shrapnel flying for miles around. By December 8, accounts were more correct, with descriptions of the fires that consumed Richmond, and details about the suburb of Richmond, with population figures in relation to those of the whole city. Little was made of the fact that a French munitions ship had been involved. It was suggested that the collision had been a German plot. The arrest of *Imo*'s helmsman, a possible spy, was given quite a bit of space. Later, the owners of *Mont Blanc* contributed $10,000 to the relief effort.

German newspapers, according to the *Chronicle Herald*, originally used the factual Reuters account, as did most foreign newspapers. Later, however, an article in a Cologne paper expressed sympathy with the people of Halifax, but stated that it was better that the munitions had not reached their destination, to be used against German troops in the trenches.

On HMS *Highflyer*, which had lost five crewmembers who reached the burning ship not long before the explosion, the first rescue work was to try to recover their bodies. Attending to the wounded and clearing up were the first priorities. A party was later sent ashore with axes and hammers. It was reported that these were left on shore. As the next few days were spent on repairs to their damaged ship, the loss of tools was significant. On December 8, a funeral party collected the bodies of the crewmembers from the official mortuary and brought them to the ship's mortuary. They were buried in Mount Olivet Cemetery.

On December 9 the captain wrote a report for the French consul. By the 10th they were ready to sail, but the convoy, whose destination was Plymouth, was delayed because of a bad storm. On December 11, HMS *Highflyer* proceeded out of the harbour, passed the buoys, and took up position to guard the convoy, where the order was to darken ship and prepare for night defence.

with spectators. Even experienced seamen on the nearby ships lined the decks. One man remarked casually, "I once saw an oil tanker burn like that. Maybe this is no place for us," but no one moved away. Families crowded the vantage points of their homes. Children on their way to school ran towards the shore to have a better view. Fort Needham provided an excellent balcony.

For nearly twenty minutes the huge column of fire from the ship floated, coming closer and closer, bringing a fog and a strange smell with it, and giving spectators plenty of time to secure the best places.

Seconds before 9:05 AM on Thursday, December 6, 1917, touching Pier 6 on the crowded Richmond shore, *Mont Blanc* exploded.

Newspaper headlines were vivid.

Halifax Herald: HALIFAX WRECKED.

Daily Express (London): APPALLING DISASTER IN CANADA. COLLISION WITH A MUNITIONS SHIP DEVASTATES THE CITY OF HALIFAX. 2000 KILLED. NOT A SINGLE HOUSE UNDAMAGED.

*Scotsman (*Edinburgh): ONE THIRD OF HALIFAX IN RUINS.

Times (London): DISASTER AT HALIFAX. CITY ON FIRE. FEARED HEAVY LOSS OF LIFE.

The disaster, for days, shared headlines with war news, such as British forces approaching Jerusalem, bombs in Bruges, the Italian Reverse, and America's declaration of war on the Austro-Hungarian Empire. The Russian Revolution was also very much in the headlines.

The headlines had not exaggerated. The whole northern part of Halifax became engulfed in a thick, sooty fog that blackened everything it touched. Shards of red hot metal showered down. When the fog lifted, the extent of the desolation and destruction was revealed.

Bewildered, not knowing what had caused this appalling wreckage, survivors did their best to save those who remained alive, or to remove bodies, hoping against hope that some life might remain. Furnaces and stoves, well stoked against winter cold, overturned. It did not take long for fire to spread through the wooden buildings, adding to the death toll and seriously hampering rescue work. A violent snowstorm hit on December 7, covering some of the wreckage but heightening the desolation. It hindered rescue work and made roads impassable.

Out of a population of some fifty thousand, two thousand, or one person in twenty-five, died. More than nine thousand were injured. The whole area that had been Richmond was left in ruins. It would take years for the people of Halifax and Dartmouth to rebuild.

The snowstorm that began on December 7 hampered rescue workers and added to the misery of the survivors in the damaged houses that still stood.

HMS *Changuinola*, an armed merchant cruiser, was anchored in mid-channel off the Dockyard. On December 7 its commanding officer, one Lieutenant Baker, wrote a report that is now available at the Public Records Office in London.

He had watched the burning ship through binoculars, and was arranging for a fire party to go ashore when the ship blew up. He sent a party ashore immediately, with orders to report to a senior officer on *Niobe* and offer assistance. He noted that the dense cloud of fog covering the area made it difficult to see what had happened, but he was convinced, because of the projectiles landing all around, that the ship had carried ammunition. At 9:30 AM, in charge of a division of men from his ship, he landed and was given orders to proceed with rescue work, which included cleaning debris and extracting bodies from the ruins. This, he reported, was made difficult owing to flames, smoke and falling timbers. Many survivors were badly injured and lived for only a few minutes. The sailors carried those who were still alive to the shore, where Lieutenant Baker obtained two tugs and had them transported to the hospital ship USS *Old Colony*.

By 2:45 PM rescue work in the burning area had become impossible, and Lieutenant Baker returned to his ship.

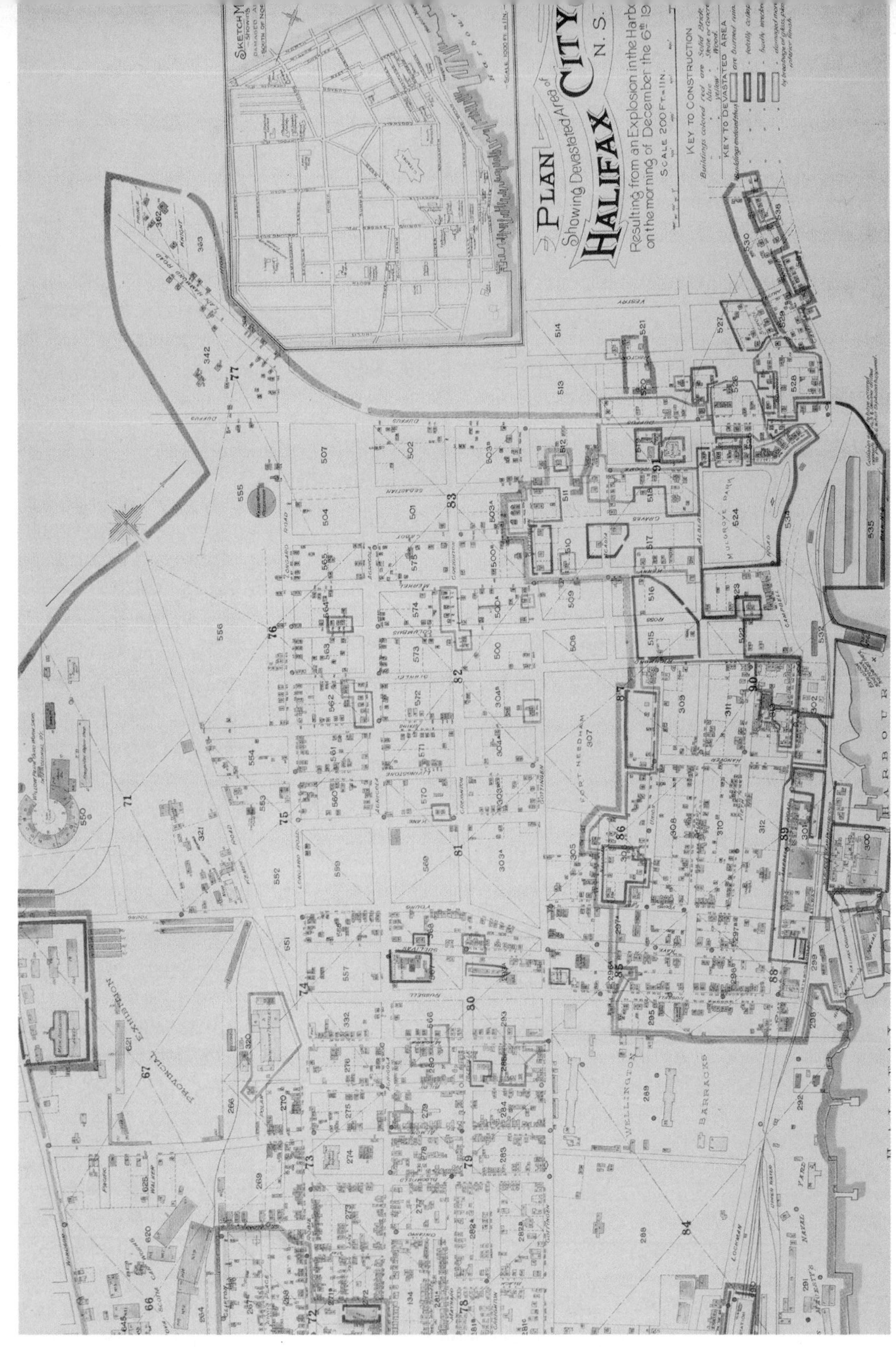

Map of devastated area

Halifax

The area of Halifax most directly affected by the explosion was Richmond, the thriving, mostly working-class area that extended up from the harbour in the northern part of the peninsula. At the time of the explosion, the street names along the harbour had recently undergone changes. Until 1917, Pleasant Street had run from Point Pleasant Park, past the Halifax Ocean Terminals, the Royal Nova Scotia Yacht Squadron, then houses and stores. At its northern end were Government House and many fine red sandstone multi-storey buildings approaching Spring Garden Road. There, the street became Barrington Street, along which the handsome buildings continued, interspersed with businesses of various kinds. On the west side were St. Paul's Church, then Victoria Square and City Hall at the corner of Duke Street. The street continued north to Cornwallis Street, where the name again changed. Now Lockman Street, it was lined with homes, grocers, Chinese laundries, butchers, barbers, a manicurist, restaurants, several boarding houses, a blacksmith, and confectioners.

After passing North Street and the train station, the street changed name once again, to Campbell Road. This meant that the railway yards were partly on Lockman Street and partly on Campbell Road. The Admiralty Grounds and Wellington Barracks followed. The street continued past the Protestant Orphans' Home, Hillis and Sons' Foundry, and the Richmond Printing Works, went through the more residential parts of Richmond, past Mulgrave Park and the Richmond Railway yards, and continued to Africville, then curved west as far as Kempt Road.

In the new city directory, published in July 1917, an innovation appeared. The whole length of the street from Point Pleasant Park to Fairview would now be Barrington, with house numbers changed accordingly. Later street changes, both in name and route, also took place. By December of the same year, people had still not become used to the new

continued on page 26

The Narrows
Barrington St
Novalea Dr
Rector St
Duffus St
Halifax Shipyards
Devonshire Ave
Lady Hammond Rd
Agricola St
Kempt Rd
Stairs St
Young St
Russell St
Robie St
Almon St
North St
Bayers Rd
Joseph Howe Dr
Oxford St
Windsor St
Connaught Ave
Mumford Rd
Chebucto Rd
Quinpool Rd
Jubilee Rd
Northwest Arm
Anchor Dr
1
2
3
4
5
6
7
8
9
10
11
12
13
14
15
16
18
19
20
21
22
23
24
25
26
27
28
29
30
31
32
33
38
44

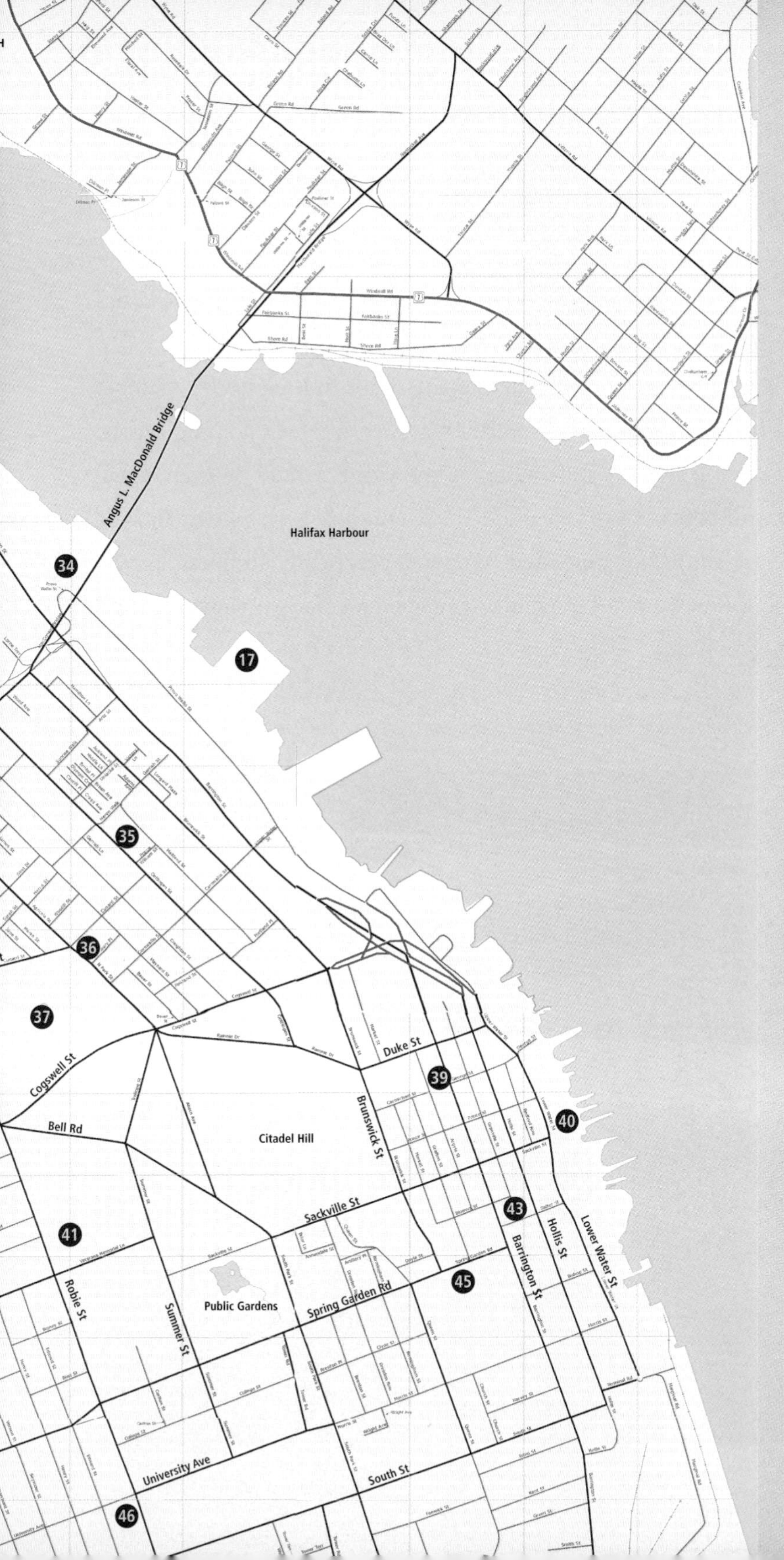

1 Fort Needham Memorial Park
2 Pier 6
3 Upham house, Rector Street
4 United Memorial Church
5 Albert Street
6 St. Joseph's Church
7 Shambhala School
8 St. Joseph's–Alexander MacKay School
9 Bloomfield School
10 Original Richmond School site
11 Former St. Joseph's Hall
12 St. Mark's Anglican Church
13 Site of Vince Coleman's house
14 Site of Richmond Yards
15 Piercey's Building Supplies
16 Protestant orphanage
17 The Naval Dockyards
18 Halifax shipyards
19 Site of Acadia Sugar Refinery
20 Site of Mulgrave Park
21 Family courthouse, former Richmond School
22 Hydrostone District
23 Hydrostone market
24 Site of Tarpaper Church
25 St. Stephen's Memorial Park
26 Firefighters' Memorial
27 Fairview Cemetery
28 Bayers Road Memorial
29 Calvin Presbyterian Church
30 Mount Olivet Cemetery
31 Regatta Point
32 Halifax Forum,
site of Dominion Exhibition grounds
33 Wellington Barracks
34 Site of North Street Station
35 Halifax North Memorial Library
36 The Armouries
37 The Commons
38 Site of Chebucto Road School
39 Grand Parade and City Hall
40 Maritime Museum of the Atlantic
41 Camp Hill Hospital
42 Site of Saint Mary's College Hospital
43 Site of YMCA Building
44 Rockhead Prison
45 Nova Scotia Technical College
46 Nova Scotia Archives
and Records Management

names, which added to the confusion of identification of people and buildings later, after so many were annihilated.

The beginning of December is usually considered the beginning of winter, and in December 1917 schools in Richmond had started their winter timetable, beginning classes at nine thirty instead of nine o'clock. There had been no real snow so far that year.

The early morning of December 6, 1917, began like any other in Richmond. As most factories operated round the clock, the streets were busy with workers coming off the night shift and others beginning the day shift. Often a few words would be exchanged, perhaps some news or a comment about the weather. The Richmond Yards, as usual, were noisy with freight cars being shifted or unloaded. Wagons, practically all horse drawn, had started their delivery rounds. Some of the motorized vehicles were already mounted on blocks for the winter.

The railway line looking north from near North Street Station

The dock area bustled with activity. A Norwegian ship lay in dry dock. Two merchant ships, SS *Calonne* and SS *Curaca*, loading with supplies for the war in Europe, were at Pier 9 and Pier 8, respectively. SS *Picton*, in for repair, stood at the Acadia Sugar Refinery dock. It carried foodstuff, with munitions in the lower hold, which was the usual British practice.

Vessels were beginning to start their daytime routine, and various whistles sounded. The British cruiser HMS *Highflyer*, in port since December 1 to escort the next convoy, had been especially well received, its sinking of a large German cruiser having made headlines in every newspaper. Its crew had been invited to all sorts of events in the city.

Homes began their daily activities. Parents filled their furnaces with coal, stoked their wood stoves, and cooked breakfast. Children prepared for school, although there were numbers of absentees at the time, because, as usual, there had been an outbreak of a childhood infectious diseases—measles and whooping cough this time. All children in affected families were in quarantine and excluded from school to try to contain the contagion. By eight thirty most children who began at nine o'clock, and even some who were going to be far too early, were ready to leave, perhaps hoping to see what was happening in the harbour that morning. The convoys were a constant source of interest, and many children had become quite expert.

On December 6 that habit of harbour watching would prove deadly, as crowds of Richmond children and adults assembled on the docks just as *Mont Blanc* exploded.

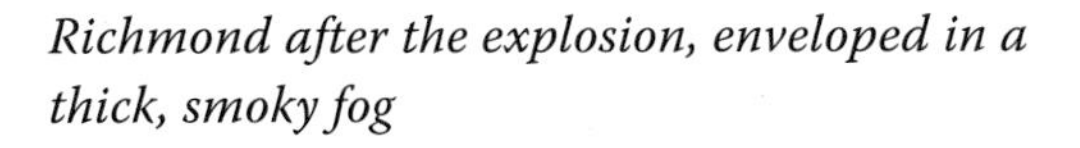

Richmond after the explosion, enveloped in a thick, smoky fog

THE SITES

Fort Needham Memorial Park

The most dramatic beginning for a tour of sites related to the Halifax Explosion is on top of Fort Needham. From the tower, looking straight down through Richmond Street towards the harbour, on the land now occupied by the shipyards of Halifax-Dartmouth Industries, once lay Pier 6, the site of the explosion.

At the time of the explosion, people were gathering on this same spot on Fort Needham. It was one of the best places to watch the drama unfold. The crowd was growing. What a sight! There were excited comments, speculation on what was burning, but no premonition of danger. Many people who stood here were injured when the explosion occurred, but were up high enough to escape the worst of the blast.

In a state of bewildered shock, they staggered helplessly, many fearing that the Germans were about to land. Gradually they dispersed to get help and to find out what had happened to their homes and families.

The monument, designed by Keith Graham, was dedicated in 1985. The design was intended to evoke the jagged ruins left by the explosion, and, with its upward thrust, hope for the future. The bells came from the United Memorial Church, built after the explosion. An extra four bells for the memorial tower were donated by Russell Isnor in 1990, enabling a wider selection of melodies to be played. Prior to that the carillon could produce "God Save the Queen," but not "O Canada."

The Halifax Explosion Memorial Bell Tower, Fort Needham Memorial Park

Objects taken from the ruins of the Upham home

Millicent (Upham) Swindells lost her mother, two sisters, a brother, and her home, and was partially blinded from the explosion. All that was found in the burnt ruins of her family's home on Rector Street were dolls' dishes, remarkably unbroken, pennies fused together by the heat, and a child's ring.

continued on page 31

Overlooking the explosion site today, as seen through the Memorial Bell Tower

The explosion site, 1917

Barbara (second from right, middle row) in 1919
at Halifax Ladies' College

Barbara stands with the bells in 1983

On the morning of December 6, Barbara Orr ran down the hill from her home on Kenny Street to ask a friend to come with her to watch the spectacle. Suddenly, all was quiet and she felt herself hurtling through the air. She landed near where the bell tower now stands, and eventually struggled to her feet. Her home was nothing but smoke and flames.

She tried to tell the frightened people who passed her that it was a ship that had blown up, but no one listened. She managed to reach her aunt's home on Gottingen Street, where the damage was bad, but there were no fires.

She found that she was unrecognizable, covered in soot and oil. Her bright red hair was no longer visible. It would be some time, after a spell in Camp Hill Hospital and numerous baths, before she regained her normal colouring. Her scars retained a blue tinge all her life. While still in hospital, she learned that her worst fears had been realized. Her whole family—mother, father, and five brothers and sisters—had been killed. The family business, the Richmond Printing Company, was in ruins. Barbara went to live with her uncle and his family, and they, like many families, did not return to live in the North End.

Later, when United Memorial Church was being built to replace two churches that had been destroyed, Barbara's uncle arranged a donation of a carillon of bells to hang in its tower in memory of her family. She pulled the great levers to play them at the opening in 1921. They remained there for over forty years, but had to be removed as the church tower could not support their weight and vibrations.

In 1984 Barbara turned the first sod for the new memorial tower. At the very moving dedication ceremony on June 9, 1985, attended by many explosion survivors pleased that an imposing monument now existed, Barbara, helped by her cousin, Bill Orr, played the bells, this time on an electronic keyboard. Prior to the construction of the monument, the bells had stood outside the church for some time. The largest bell has an inscription reading, "In Memoriam. Samuel Orr and his wife Annie S. Orr, and their children, Ian, Mary, Archie, Isabel and James, who departed this life December 6, 1917. Presented by their daughter Barbara, 1920."

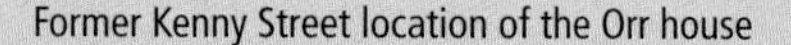

Former Kenny Street location of the Orr house

continued from page 29

In a niche inside the Halifax Explosion memorial is a time capsule with material from 1917 and from 1985, inserted by Millicent Swindells. It is due to be opened on December 6, 2017. It is anticipated that Millicent's granddaughter who accompanied her will be present. Memorial services are held each December 6, beginning before 9:00 AM, with a minute's silence at the time of the explosion. The bells ring out, playing "O God, Our Help in Ages Past" and "Abide with Me."

The original fort on Needham Hill was a small earthen redoubt with some wooden structures, constructed by Captain William Spry in 1778 for the defence of the dockyard. There is now little sign of military strongholds, but there are various monuments.

One such monument is a small cairn on the hill, a reminder that Captain James Cook, the great explorer also known for his travel in the Pacific regions, spent time in Halifax in 1761–62, carrying out a survey of Halifax Harbour. Fort Needham was considered a suitable site for a monument, as it overlooks the harbour.

Halifax Relief Commission monument

To the south, past the playing field and tennis courts, on its own grassy meadow, stands the Halifax Relief Commission monument. The commission was founded on January 22, 1918, by an Order-in-Council of the Canadian government to administer relief funds and restore the area affected by the explosion. It took over relief efforts that had previously been handled by the various relief committees.

The commission consisted of a prominent lawyer as chairman, a judge, and an Oshawa businessman. A local businessman, already involved in relief work, was appointed secretary.

One of the first tasks was to cover the cost of funeral and medical expenses for victims, and then to make living allowances for widows, orphans, the seriously injured, particularly

The Halifax Relief Commission monument

those who had been blinded or had lost limbs, and those left without means. The commission provided temporary and later permanent housing.

Property loss had to be assessed, appraisals and claims judged, for businesses as well as private homes. Claims varied from household goods, like fifteen bottles of pickles at $4.50, to $190,000 for the loss of the Acadia Sugar Refinery. Eventually pensions were paid to widows and orphans, and for permanent injuries such as the loss of limbs or blindness. For less serious injuries or loss, the victim had a choice of a lump sum or a pension. The commission organized reconstruction, sometimes expropriating land for the new roads and buildings necessary for a community to be re-established. It came in for a great deal of criticism and complaint at times, but remained firm in its decisions. It employed numbers of people and had its own offices, temporary ones at first, and later permanent ones at the corner of Isleville and Young streets, in a hydrostone building. Social work was an important task: the commission kept in touch with all pensioners and supervised orphans until they were adults. It also collected rent for the Hydrostone stores and homes.

By 1919 the commission was down to two members, their salary decreased from $7,500 to $1,875. A permanent secretary, a returned army officer named William Tibbs, was put in charge of the day-to-day running of the commission. By 1929 it employed only one social worker. The number of commissioners varied, sometimes two, occasionally three, but there were remarkably few during the commission's fifty-eight years, as most remained for life.

The commission was ended on June 11, 1976. Two pensioners remain as of May 2006; their monthly allowance is now paid by the Department of Veterans' Affairs.

The monument names commissioners, but only up till 1950. On the other side, a plaque tells of the establishment of Fort Needham as a memorial park developed by the relief commission "in memory of those known and unknown who suffered." It was the commission that created the playing fields and picnic area, spending over $165,000 before handing the park over to the city in 1957.

cup that remained
ct in the ruins of the
e Street Methodist
rch manse

Kaye Street Methodist Church and United Memorial Church

A path leads from Fort Needham Park to Needham Street, which is crossed by Young Street. This part was known as East Young Street in 1917. On the block between East Young and Kaye streets lay Kaye Street Methodist Church. Its minister was the Reverend William Swetnam.

Just before 9:00 AM on December 6, the Swetnam family was in the living room of the manse. The two children, Carmen and Dorothy, normally attended school at the Protestant Orphanage, but Dorothy was just recovering from whooping cough, and so neither was allowed to attend school in case of spreading the infection. Mrs. Swetnam was playing the piano, to accompany Carmen, who was rehearsing his song for the Christmas concert. Dorothy lay curled in a chair, while Mr. Swetnam stood in the doorway, observing.

Kaye Street Methodist Church

Suddenly the peaceful scene changed. The house collapsed. The piano toppled. The roof caved in. Mr. Swetnam was not badly hurt, but he could find no signs of life in his wife, nor in his son. Then he heard Dorothy crying. She was pinned down by heavy boards. When he tried to shift them, it hurt her more, and he stopped. Then a neighbour came in. "The house is starting to burn!" she called out. Not caring now if it did hurt her more, he and the neighbour sawed at the boards and heaved them off the little girl, now screaming with pain, and got themselves away from the flames already licking the timbers.

Found in the ruins of the manse was a delicate china cup, without a chip. The handle is an angel. The words read, "Remember me."

Eight-year-old Dorothy wrote a long letter to her aunt a few days later. She added, "PS Mummy and Carmen are dead. Dorothy and Daddy are alive."

This house is typical of the pre-explosion houses near the Methodist church. It was on Albert Street, in the burnt out area. Very often houses in Richmond were built of wood and usually had a flat roof. Along sections of the main streets, like Barrington Street, there were row houses, some rented as apartments, some housing individual families. Throughout the area there were single-family homes, usually two storeys, with picket-fenced yards. Families might keep a few chickens or even a cow. Many grew vegetables. Certain streets contained more semi-detached houses with two families or two apartments. Stables were not uncommon, many gradually being converted for automobiles.

Albert Street was one of the longer streets with a variety of houses. Most were single family. There were three small stores, one selling confectionery, and the others groceries.

The United Memorial Church now stands on part of the foundations of Kaye Street Methodist Church. The sadly depleted congregations of Kaye Street Methodist and Grove Presbyterian on Duffus Street worshipped in a temporary tarpaper church nearby on Young Street until the new church was ready. Between them the two churches had lost 239 parishioners. The new church was originally to be known as the Kaye/Grove Church. In

Pre-explosion house on Albert Street

June 1920 the union was officially recognized, creating a forerunner of the United Church of Canada, which was established in 1925. The United Memorial Church's opening was celebrated in 1921, when the carillon, played by a very nervous Barbara Orr, rang from its tower. A mistake would have been heard all over the neighbourhood. The newspaper report described a wonderful tune. Inside are windows and other memorials and photographs relating to the history of the church and congregation, including the names of the parishioners who died. The entrance has an inscription that reads:

1920
UNITED MEMORIAL CHURCH
FORMERLY
KAYE STREET METHODIST AND GROVE
PRESBYTERIAN
IN MEMORY OF MEMBERS AND ADHERENTS,
WHO ON ACCOUNT OF THE EXPLOSION,
DECEMBER 6, 1917, ENTERED INTO REST

United Memorial Church

Grove Presbyterian Church was too badly damaged to be rebuilt. Ironically, a celebration had taken place in the church hall on the evening of December 5, at which the mortgage had been ceremonially burnt. The building was now free of debt. The minister, Mr. Crowdis, and his family lived on Gottingen Street. Their house collapsed towards the harbour, showing the effects of explosion and implosion, but did not catch fire. Mr. Crowdis had been watching the drama from Fort Needham. This was his description: "Jets of flame and spiral puffs of smoke shot heavenwards." When he returned home he found his house collapsed, his wife and sisters-in-law injured, his children not seriously hurt, but frightened and bewildered. His wife had facial injuries and lost one eye.

Grove Presbyterian Church, pre-explosion

St. Joseph's (Church and Schools)

Between Kaye Street and Russell Street, on the corner of Gottingen Street, stands St. Joseph's Roman Catholic Church. The present building dates from 1959. It contains colourful stained glass windows, designed to reflect the church's history. In 1917 the church on Gottingen Street, the convent, and the glebe house for the priest, Father McManus, round the corner on Russell Street, were very badly damaged. The newly installed pipe organ, which added greatly to the enjoyment of the services, was destroyed. Subsequently, the church basement was used for worship until the present building was inaugurated. In 1992 a special memento was produced depicting the present church and a sandstone chip from the original church.

St. Joseph's Church discontinued services at the end of June 2006 for reasons of economy, and members were requested to attend St. Stephen's Church on Normandy Drive. What is in store for the church building is still an open question.

In Richmond, children attended school in accordance with their religious faith. Roman Catholics were further divided according to their sex. There was compulsory education from age five or six to age fifteen, but with special permission, because of family hardship requiring another wage to help out, a student might leave at age fourteen.

St. Joseph's Church after the explosion

St. Joseph's Church before the explosion

St. Joseph's Girls' School, a Catholic school on Kaye Street, had 447 on its roll in grades one through eight. In 1917, there were 110 in grade one, and 19 in grade eight. Numbers had increased since before the war, making it necessary for one class to use the stage of the auditorium. Most of the teachers were Sisters of Charity, who wore habits at that time. Music lessons were given at the convent nearby. Every morning began with prayers at nine o'clock.

The Catholic boys' school had been on Young Street, but it burned down. While the new school was under construction, the 373 boys shared the St. Joseph's building, alternating weekly by having either morning or afternoon sessions. Among the boys, there were 115 in grade one and 10 in grade eight.

St. Joseph's Girls' School before the explosion

St. Joseph's-Alexander MacKay School today

St. Joseph's after the explosion

A class at St. Joseph's Girls' School before the explosion

At St. Joseph's Girls' School, four girls were killed and four later died in hospital, but they were safer in the sturdier school building than in their own wooden houses. Fifteen students died at home. The girls are pictured here wearing their "tire," as they called their uniforms. Note the large number in a class.

The Catholic boys, due to attend the same school in the afternoon, were at home or outside. Fifty-five boys lost their lives. No teachers were killed, but several were injured.

The present St Joseph's–Alexander MacKay School, on Russell Street, occupies roughly the same site as the former St. Joseph's School.

Nearby on the corner of Gottingen and Russell streets the new boys' school was almost complete. Named for an educator, Alexander MacKay, it was damaged, but still able to be set up as a temporary food depot by the appropriate relief committee.

In the 1970s St. Joseph's School and Alexander MacKay School merged and became coeducational. A sister who taught there at the time said that she was worried about teaching boys, but found that the mixed classes worked well. In 1995, the Alexander MacKay building was sold by the city to the Shambhala Buddhist organization and became Shambhala School.

People line up for food at Alexander MacKay School

The Shambhala School

Richmond School, a Protestant school on Roome Street, had a roll of 421 students in seven classrooms, usually with over 60 in each. With the increase in population because of the war, there were 94 students in grade one. By contrast there were only 9 students in grade nine because of early leavers, but they studied high school subjects: Latin, algebra, physics. Some of them would go on to Bloomfield High School, not far away on Bloomfield Street. Mr. Huggins, the principal, also trained the Richmond School Cadets, famous for their smartness and drill. They had won national prizes.

The boys of Richmond School, diving off Pier 6 in summer 1917

There was also a one-room school at the Protestant Orphanage on Veith Street, and a very small number of non-orphans whose parents had connections with the orphanage, and who lived close by, were pupils there. Miss Dexter, the only teacher, was in charge of the education of sixty-seven children, in grades one through four.

Bloomfield School, with its two buildings, the common school and the high school, was at the corner of Bloomfield and Agricola streets. It was damaged, the junior school seriously, but the casualty rate was much lower than at the other schools. Its students lived further from the totally

Class of Richmond School survivors

devastated area. The school, with added buildings, has for the last fifteen years been the Bloomfield Centre, with rooms rented to various community organizations.

In all, four school buildings, Richmond, St. Joseph's, Bloomfield Common, and the Protestant Orphanage School, were destroyed.

Richmond School was rebuilt on a new site, and Mr. Huggins, who had lost his daughter and been injured in the explosion, continued as principal but remained only a short time.

A Richmond School reunion took place in 1984. One classroom was set aside for the class of 1917. A large number of explosion survivors attended. Some bore the permanent scars and injuries caused by the blast. As remembrances were shared, and photographs shown, there was sadness, and tears blurred the eyes, but there was also laughter, especially at the old class groups.

The old desks and blackboards brought back memories, and there was a great deal of talk of the school that was destroyed, and of its students and teachers. Two years later, in October 1986, the school was converted to the family courthouse.

On the opposite side of Gottingen Street from Alexander MacKay School, number 2882, the former St. Joseph's Hall was damaged but repaired and used as a supply depot. For many years it was used by a flooring contractor, whose name appears on the building, although recently, the owner has changed.

St. Joseph's Hall in 2005

St. Joseph's Hall in 1917

St. Mark's Church

St. Mark's Church with the Royal Canadian Regiment

On Russell Street, on the same side as St. Joseph's School, is St. Mark's Anglican Church, where the first services took place in 1921, when the archbishop dedicated the memorials. An article in the *Mail Star* stated, "Inevitably some sadness, since memory will be busy, will mingle with the joy of the opening service."

The original church, over a block from the present building, stood on the corner of Russell and Albert streets, adjacent to Wellington Barracks. Consecrated in 1866, it was twice enlarged to provide seating for the military and naval personnel who formed a large part of the congregation. Church parades were a common and colourful sight. At one time, a goat, a regimental mascot, would spend its time in the Sunday school building during the service. Fire completed the explosion's destruction of St. Mark's.

The present-day St. Mark's Church

Vince Coleman's home

Further down Russell Street, past the former site of St. Mark's, diagonally opposite on the corner stood 31 Russell Street, home of Vince Coleman. He was the train dispatcher at the Richmond Yards. The Richmond Yards dealt mostly with freight, but also with passengers to a lesser degree. Most of the employees on duty at the time of the explosion were killed. Vince Coleman, instead of rushing out of his office when he learned of the burning ship's cargo, stayed behind to send a message: "Munitions ship on fire in the harbour. Making for Pier 6. Goodbye." He died on duty but saved many lives by warning the

The site of Vince Coleman's home

approaching passenger train. The equipment he used is on display at the Maritime Museum of the Atlantic.

The house shown here was built on the site of the Coleman house. The Richmond Yards, which were near Duffus Street, now on North Marginal Road, are now part of the Scotia Terminals. The foundations of one end of a pedestrian bridge, built to enable workers to cross the railway lines safely, are still visible. The first train to reach the city on December 6, 1917, had to stop before it reached the Richmond Yards. Its passengers were shocked by what met them when they tried to walk to Halifax. The train later left for Truro.

Richmond Printing Company

To the left, just past Kaye Street, was located the Richmond Printing Company, owned by Samuel Orr and his two sons, Samuel and David.

The Richmond Printing Company had been started by William McTaggart Orr in 1896, in a bedroom of his father's house on Kenny Street, in Richmond, with a hand press, some type, a few cases, some cardboard, and capital of thirty-six dollars. He was later joined by his brothers, Samuel and David.

Searching the ruins of the Richmond Printing Company

By 1910 he had become so successful that he purchased a block of land on the railway line near the dry dock on Young Street. There, the Richmond Printing Company, a two-storey building both sturdy and fireproof, was constructed of granite blocks. But it was not explosion-proof. Thirty-eight people, including David Orr, were killed when the building collapsed. Samuel Orr died on his way to work. William was badly injured, and taken to the American hospital ship *Old Colony*, not returning to his distraught family for several days.

The company did not return to Richmond. After a brief spell on Hollis Street, downtown, it moved to permanent premises on Kempt Road, where it was called the Richmond Paper Company.

By 1942 a son, William Orr, known as Bill, managed the business. There were three disastrous fires, but the company prospered. Not long after William McTaggart Orr died, in 1960, the firm was taken over by Domtar, with Bill Orr remaining as manager until he retired in 1976.

Dominion Textile Factory

Another factory with many employees, the Dominion Textile Factory, was also destroyed, although it was further from the harbour, on Robie Street. The company rebuilt on the site of the present Piercey's Building Supplies.

The Dominion Textile Factory after the explosion

Piercey's Building Supplies

Protestant Orphanage

On the other side of Young Street, between Barrington and Veith streets, are Veith House, the replacement for the Protestant Orphanage, and the Wee Care Centre for children with special needs. A plaque on the Veith Street side tells of the Protestant Orphanage that occupied this site.

The 1875 report of the orphanage's board of governors noted that the building was "large and airy, having an excellent basement." The 1878 report stated that the grounds were large enough that "the children can play and take exercise without going into the public thoroughfare."

On the morning of December 6, 1917, the matron did not like the sounds coming from the harbour, and, thinking that her charges might be in danger, she ordered them all to hurry to that excellent basement. It did not suffice. She, her assistant, a housemaid, and twenty-five children lost their lives. The buildings were destroyed.

The four trees planted in memory of the Ross children

In the grounds, near the fence on the north side are four trees and stone markers in memory of the four Ross children—Clifford, six months old; Doris, three years; Freddie, five; and Eileen, seven—who died at their home at 9 Duffus Street. Their father was an engineer on board *Niobe.* Both he and the mother survived. It was almost eighty years later

The grounds of the Protestant Orphanage after the explosion

Veith House today

HMCS Niobe

that a descendant of the family, with the help of the Halifax Foundation, arranged for the trees and stones. On May 7, 1999, at a memorial service, he planted the trees.

A total of 155 people perished on Veith Street.

Between Barrington Street and the harbour stretch the Dockyards, where various ships lie at anchor. In 1917 HMCS *Niobe*, a Canadian navy cruiser, was permanently moored at the Dockyard. With added superstructure, it was used as a training and depot ship, and held the offices of naval control and intelligence. HMCS *Niobe* sustained damage in the explosion, but as the ship was built for war, the damage was repairable. *Niobe* continued to fulfil its wartime functions.

Dockyard

In 1917 the dockyard area was occupied by His Majesty's Naval Yard, with its dry dock and wharves, and part by the Acadia Sugar Refinery. The Dockyard contained various buildings, barracks, workshops,

A special Children's Committee was formed shortly after December 6. The committee's priorities included seeing to urgent repairs to children's institutions, investigating homes where children were receiving care, hunting for lost children, identifying "unclaimed" children, and various other problems. The numbers are shocking: 200 required serious hospital treatment; 70 were orphaned; 120 lost their mother; 180 their father; 7 had been blinded; 48 suffered a serious eye injury. In 111 cases, the father was serving overseas. Where there were close relatives willing and suitable to supply a home, orphans were placed with them, but that still left a large number to be considered.

Some four hundred letters from all over Canada and the United States poured in with offers to adopt. Some were specific, requesting good Scotch or Irish parentage, children without physical deformities or serious injury, or girls of about fourteen willing to do housework. A letter from Tennessee requested a child who was "not from an unrefined family." Some letters from rural areas made requests for boys of twelve to fourteen, who could help on the farm. Many gave references from their church, and some were definite about religion. Finally, it was decided that orphaned children should stay close to Halifax so that they could be properly supervised. So the city's orphanages—the Catholic one on Quinpool Road, the Home of the Guardian Angel on Brunswick Street, the Protestant Orphanage in its temporary quarters in the Nova Scotia Yacht Squadron building near Point Pleasant Park, and the infants' home on Tower Road—all received explosion orphans.

The Halifax Relief Commission and its social workers supervised explosion orphans carefully. The monthly pension paid for each orphan was $16 and continued to age seventeen.

Dockyard Sign

repair sheds, and stores. In 1889, the large dry dock had been built for the use of the Royal Navy, but soon merchant ships in for repair took advantage of its facilities.

Also in the Dockyard in 1917, in a red sandstone building, was the Royal Naval College of Canada, attended by boys training to become naval officers. They were resident, and subject to strict regulations, rising at 6:30 AM, then exercise and cold baths, followed by breakfast and an hour free between 8:05 and 9:05. Then a bell rang for cleaning up.

On the morning of December 6, before free time ended, someone shouted that he could see a fire to the north. The smoke and flame had reached a great height, even above the tall sugar refinery. However, the bell rang and they obeyed bells.

George Mitchell, a junior cadet at the time, had just reached the junior gun room when the explosion happened. He immediately thought that it had to be an explosion, and that it was on a ship. He knew that a lot of ships carried ammunition. The boys rushed outside. It was as if small hail was coming down. It did not sting, but it made a noise. There was a great mushroom cloud of smoke.

They were lined up and told to disperse. Where? George decided to go home. He had a cut on his upper lip; a piece of glass had somehow got beneath his coat sleeve, and there was blood there too. He walked as if in shock, hardly aware of his surroundings. He reached his home on Tower Road, went to bed for a while, and received medical attention at Pine Hill Hospital. For the rest of his life, loud, unexpected noises made him jump.

The Royal Naval College did not return to the Dockyard; it was moved to Kingston, Ontario.

Two buildings in the yard were completely destroyed, all others seriously damaged. Twenty-one of the naval personnel died.

In June 1918, the Halifax Shipyards set up a large shipbuilding plant north of the Dockyard on some of the land left empty of industry because of the explosion. These yards and the dry dock are still very much used.

Acadia Sugar Refinery

The Acadia Sugar Refinery, the tallest building east of Montreal, outstanding in all photographs of the city until 1917, employed over a hundred men at the time of its highest production. That number had shrunk by 1917, as the refinery had been put up for sale, and some of the work was already transferred to the Dartmouth refinery.

On that Thursday morning, the spectacular burning ship, drawing ever closer to shore, caused a great deal of excitement. Practically all of the men climbed up to the open rooftop to have the best possible view.

Very few survived. The mechanical superintendent was Vincent Pattison. It took time for those massive ruins to be cleared, and Pattison's body was not found until April 1918. His

The Acadia Sugar Refinery before the explosion

Vincent Pattison and children, outside their home on Gottingen Street, c. 1915.

The Acadia Sugar Refinery (far right) and ruins after the explosion

Dry dock holding Hovland

oldest son, almost sixteen by then, was able to identify the watch worn by his father. Borrowed from his brother James, who kept it a little fast, it had stopped forever at ten minutes after nine. Vincent Pattison was not to know that his two youngest children had also been killed, his wife badly injured, and his home on north Barrington Street (which belonged to the Sugar Refinery) left a burned-out wreck.

The Norwegian ship *Hovland* was in the Graving dock at the time of the explosion. All crewmembers were on board, since, as neutrals, they were not allowed ashore. Five of the crew were killed.

Hillis and Sons' Foundry

Hillis and Sons' Foundry lay not far from the refinery. A piece of its wall can still be seen. Few of these workers survived. Richard Powell, with the cross above his head was killed, his body never found. His little daughter also died. She had whooping cough at the time of the explosion, and exposure caused pneumonia. The president of the foundry, Frank Hillis, died there. The foundry was completely wrecked and never rebuilt.

Hillis & Sons' Foundry

A row of two-storey tenement houses lined Barrington Street, between Ross and Kenny streets. Owned by Thomas Flinn, and locally known as the Flinn Block, it consisted of rented apartments and one boarding house, where most of the rooms were occupied by men working on the docks.

Of the twelve families that lived on the block, forty-five of the residents were killed, with four children orphaned and others left with only one parent. Two families were completely wiped out. Thomas Flinn, his sister, and his housekeeper died. The buildings collapsed and caught fire, making identification of the remains and personal belongings among the ruins even more difficult.

Later social workers' reports reflected the tragedy. "Depressed, shocked, run down," was the description of one woman, who had lost all four children. Her husband was overseas, and leave was not immediately granted. It was a sad homecoming for such men. One, whose love letters to his wife were salvaged from the ruins of the building, said that it was difficult for him to submit a claim for lost possessions, as he did not know how his wife had furnished her apartment. Some of her bills, including an agreement to pay for a sewing machine over a number of months, had survived, but were in the wrong mortuary bag. It was difficult for workers sifting through wreckage to

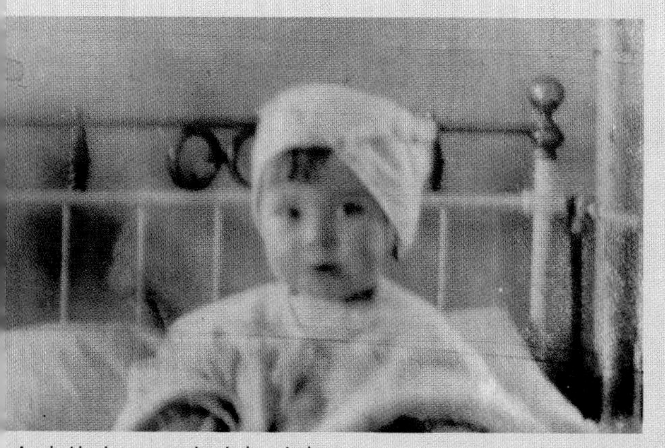

Annie Liggins recovering in hospital

The street on which Annie Liggins and her family lived after the explosion.

attribute belongings correctly. Another report noted that, for the two surviving children and the mother in a family where the father and other children had been killed, the clothing supplied by the relief committee was totally unsuitable, as it was coloured. A son in that family said that, all her life, his mother would not talk about the explosion, but, as December 6 approached, she would become silent and unhappy.

One survival amazed everyone who saw the devastated building. A man whose family had lived there was searching the area. His wife had been dug out after five hours, but five of his children were still missing. He thought he heard a sound, and called for help. Soldiers rushed over. A little girl lay there, obviously still alive. An ash pan had fallen on top of her, and saved her life. She had been there for twenty-six hours. At first it was assumed that she belonged to his family, but an aunt visiting the hospital recognized the young child. She was just two years old, injured, and had not given her surname. She was Annie Liggins. Her mother and brother were killed, her father was serving overseas. The sergeant in charge of the party that dug her out must have been very pleased with the miraculous rescue, as he visited her in hospital and took photographs, one of which he gave to Annie. On the back of the photo is written, "Annie Liggins (Ashpan baby). Rescued after being buried for 26 hr under debris of house. Compliments of Co. Sergeant Major Davies. Machine Gunner. 63rd HR."

Pier 6

The site of *Mont Blanc*'s explosion, between Richmond Street and Ross Street, where Pier 6 stood in 1917, now lies just off the dockyard. Ross Street no longer exists, but in 1917 six families lived there. Nine people were killed.

The site of the former Pier 6

Mulgrave Park

A park favoured by the citizens of Richmond has disappeared, but its name lives on in Mulgrave Park Baptist Church on Sebastian Street. Originally bounded by Barrington, Duffus, Albert, and Richmond streets, Mulgrave Park was popular for picnicking in summer, as well as for skating on its pond and tobogganing on the steep streets on either side of it in winter. In the early days the park grounds held a grove of beech trees, watercourses, and a reservoir. By 1917 some of the lands had been sold for housing, but the park, although less than half its original size, retained its leisure uses.

The Manning Pool, built on Mulgrave Park by the architects of Wartime Housing Limited, housed officers and men of the merchant marine awaiting their ships for the crossing of the Atlantic during the Second World War.

A public housing project, opened in 1961, consists of twenty-two low-rise buildings and two eight-storey apartment buildings; in 2002 three-storey maisonnettes were added.

Public housing where Mulgrave Park once stood

Just across Roome Street from Mulgrave Park, on Barrington Street, was a store much frequented by the people of Richmond. Isaac Creighton and Co. carried a large selection of groceries, dry goods, and the like. The "and Co." were Isaac's sons, William and Campbell ("Cam," for short). The top floor provided a spacious home for Isaac and his family.

On the morning of the explosion, Cam had left the store and gone right down to the waterfront to have an even closer look at the fire in the harbour. When the ship exploded, he, surprisingly, received no serious injuries and rushed back to the store, which was now a pile of wreckage. He managed to extricate his younger brother, Austin, from the debris. Then he heard cries, and recognized a young woman who worked for them. He tried to lift the large beams that pinned her, but they were too cumbersome for him. "I can see daylight now. I'll run and get help!" he shouted to her. Just then, the flames flared throughout the building, and he was forced to retreat. He was sure that his wife, his father, mother, and sister were already dead, but that girl was certainly alive. Her screams haunted him for the rest of his life. As he made his way to safety, he found his horse, driven frantic and obviously blinded. By this time a few soldiers had appeared, and he did what he thought was the kindest thing: he asked a soldier to shoot the poor animal.

Cam stayed with his Creighton cousins on LeMarchant Street, along with other relatives, the Grants, who had lost everything and their home on Veith Street. They too had been watching the drama. Mrs. Grant's sister, Mary, remarked, "I am sorry it happened, but I'm glad I am here to see it." She was tall and kindly wrapped her arms around a small neighbour, who was shivering, as she had not had the forethought to bring a coat. The excitement was too great. Mary was killed, but the little woman survived, unhurt.

Dr. G. W. I. Creighton with past Lieutenant-Governor of Nova Scotia, Her Honour Myra Freeman

The house on LeMarchant Street, although much further south, had lost doors and windows. A next-door neighbour known to be very houseproud was crying, "My house is ruined."

"Are your children all right?" Graham Creighton asked.

"I think so."

"Then keep quiet about your house," he ordered as he went about finding how he could fix up windows and doors. Graham Creighton was a man of stature, a school inspector for Halifax City and County.

His fourteen-year-old son, Wilfred, accompanied Cam on a walk back to Richmond, to rescue what they could from the Grant house on Veith Street. A later report in the *Daily Echo* told of Cam Creighton, "deprived of home and relatives at one stroke.... Friends were surprised that he had enough 'kick' left...to set up the old business on a new site....The store is at a corner where Spring after Spring years ago, the old Merkle farm blossomed abundantly and fall after fall gave their bumper crop....A refrigerator with several airtight thickness and the best of sanitary appointments with meat of various kinds." Pictures that remain in Dr. Wilfred Creighton's mind are of dead horses, the fire engine "Patricia," and the scant remains of the Creighton store opposite Mulgrave Park, where there had been beech trees, quoit beds, and benches. He can still conjure up the smell that pervaded the whole area.

Richmond School

In December 1917 Richmond School, like other schools in the neighbourhood, had begun its winter timetable, starting half an hour later than usual, at 9:30 AM. The school was badly damaged. Two students died in the schoolyard and eighty-six others died at home or outside, many of them watching the spectacle in the harbour.

After the explosion, the Halifax Relief Commission appointed Thomas Adams, a British town planner, to lead the reconstruction of the devastated area. One of his innovations was the creation of new streets that followed the natural contours of the land, in contrast with Richmond's grid pattern. Two streets—Devonshire Avenue and Dartmouth Avenue—were built as broad boulevards, meeting at a forty-five-degree angle. Approached from Richmond Street, Devonshire Avenue curves round Fort Needham.

The pre-explosion Richmond School

The Richmond School ruins

Close to where the two new streets cross, the rebuilt Richmond School, now the family courthouse, was completed in 1921. The name "Richmond School" still appears above the door. Inside is a display of explosion-related photographs.

Rockhead Prison, in use since 1861, was closed at the end of 1969, when the prisoners were moved to Sackville and the land was made available for development.

The rebuilt Richmond School in almost empty surroundings, with Rockhead Prison on the hilltop

Hydrostone district

After intersecting with Dartmouth Avenue, Devonshire Avenue joins the continuation of Gottingen Street, renamed Novalea Drive in 1981. Here, also bordered by Isleville, from Young Street to Duffus Street, begin the blocks of houses built and rented by the Halifax Relief Commission to replace homes that had been destroyed. The development was planned by Thomas Adams and was inspired by the "garden city" philosophy, as evidenced by the broad, tree-lined boulevards and the rear laneways. The houses were designed by George Ross, of the Montreal firm of Ross and Macdonald, and constructed of hydrostone, a type of cement block. People were interested in this fire-resistant building material, which was new in Halifax. There was, however, quite a bit of local opposition to the new roads, some of which had less steep gradients, and to the hydrostone development, which was considered too fanciful. A public meeting, where plans were shown, was the scene of some heated objections about the roads and the ideas for reconstruction. Many wanted their old Richmond returned to them, their old way of life brought back. But the Relief Commission went ahead. Imaginative names for the new neighbourhood were suggested, including "Merkelsfield," but the development came to be known simply as the Hydrostone. The blocks

Former Richmond School, now a family courthouse

Furniture from the Massachusetts-Halifax Relief Fund

were made in Eastern Passage, and a special railway line was constructed to transport them from the docks.

The first 24 dwellings in the Hydrostone district were ready for occupation in March 1919, with 20 more to be finished every two weeks. Labour disputes slowed progress, but by 1921 all 324 units were completed. Soon some two thousand people were living there. Monthly rents ranged from twenty-five dollars for a four-room flat to fifty dollars for a seven-room house.

The row of stores on Young Street was also part of the plan. Originally, there were two clothing stores (Colwell Brothers and Nielson and Mills), a bank, a shoe store, a pharmacy, a furniture store, a grocer, a tobacconist, branch offices of the local newspaper, and the Halifax Relief Commission's headquarters. Rent for the commercial properties ranged from $55.00 to $134.50.

The living room of the hydrostone house above, photographed in 1988, was still furnished with furniture from the Massachusetts relief supplies. After the explosion, money and relief supplies had come in from far and wide. But what stood out in the memories of explosion sufferers was the unstinting generosity of the State of Massachusetts. In goods

The newly completed Hydrostone in September 1921

and money its government donated over $750,000 to what became the Massachusetts–Halifax Relief Fund.

As soon as word of the tragedy reached Boston, about two hours after the explosion, the state governor sent a telegram offering unlimited assistance. A public safety committee of about a hundred members existed, prepared for disaster. By ten o'clock that evening they had a train to transport thirteen surgeons and doctors, nurses, railway officials, and medical supplies. That was just the beginning. The state set up a hospital staffed with medical and social workers, and sent huge quantities of supplies of every kind, including a warehouse full of household goods on Windsor Street. This was new, not used furniture, and those in need could choose from a wide variety of styles, as if they were in a store. Some of this furniture can still be found in homes throughout the North End.

By the time the Halifax Relief Commission moved to permanent offices in the Hydrostone district, most of the immediate relief and compensation had been dealt with. However, the commission continued to pay pensions to widows, orphans, and the permanently disabled, and to employ social workers who monitored the welfare of survivors. The commission also collected rent for the Hydrostone properties.

The effects of Halifax's economic depression were delayed by relief money, but by the mid-twenties many of the stores in the Hydrostone were empty, and some of the homes not occupied. The commission refused to reduce rents. One survivor who lived in the Hydrostone talked of empty houses and broken windows. The outbreak of the

The *Evening Echo* of February 10, 1921, printed essays written by pupils of the Alexander MacKay and Richmond schools who were living in the Hydrostone. Extracts follow:

"We are not afraid to go to sleep because of the fire, and we don't have to wade through mud up to our necks. We like the new shopping district.... The boulevards are pretty, but I have one fault to find with houses, that is that they are too small." The girl who expressed these ideas was the daughter of Constant Upham, killed when he remained to warn others of danger. His store and home were wrecked.

"The houses are fireproof and warm.... The garbage man comes every Friday. The new Richmond School...will be the finest in Eastern Canada. It will have a library. I think it will be lovely."

"I like my new home. I am not afraid of the fire in the night there. The streets are cement.... There are dry goods and groceries and drug stores. The houses are nice inside." The boy who wrote this essay had lost his home, his father, and his brother in the disaster.

Second World War in 1939 brought renewed prosperity, as Halifax was again a war base, and accommodation was at a premium. In 1949 the relief commission began selling its properties: $2,500 for an apartment, $3,500 for a larger house. By 1955 sales were completed, though the commission kept its offices and a few units. When the commission ceased to exist in June 1976, its offices were sold to the federal government. Remaining funds for the payment of pensions were entrusted to the Department of Veterans' Affairs. In 2006 survivors were still receiving pensions.

All of the Hydrostone stores and offices are now fully occupied and are a popular place to shop. They have come to be known as the Hydrostone Market. The Hydrostone district has become a fashionable neighbourhood. Some of the buildings are now covered with wooden or vinyl siding, but many retain their original finish. In addition, individual houses made of

Young Street, not far from the present-day Hydrostone district, just after the explosion

The Hydrostone Market today

The Hydrostone stores in the early 1920s, with the Halifax Relief Commission offices at the end of the block

hydrostone can be found scattered throughout the area that was rebuilt after the explosion.

In the grassy space opposite the Hydrostone Market, where the tarpaper church stood after the explosion, there is a small display, with diagrams and explanations of the development. The Hydrostone is believed to be the earliest English-style garden suburb, and the oldest planned community of any kind, in Canada.

The tarpaper church

In 1917 the grocery store of W. I. Hubley and Company stood at the corner of Gottingen and Kaye streets. It escaped major damage and was reopened. The present store, although sporting a different name, is in the original building.

The contemporary display

St. Stephen's

On Normandy Drive, a block north of Duffus Street, near where it crosses Robie, is St. Stephen's Memorial Park, where there is a piece of metal thought to be from *Mont Blanc* and a splinter from the first St. Joseph's Church. Until a few years ago this park looked a little neglected and could easily be passed by. But then some parishioners decided to remedy that. The result is an interesting, beautifully maintained, colourful place with flower beds, the monuments all restored and mounted where necessary for preservation. A few of the church members continue their diligent care. They can be seen painting, changing and improving flower beds appropriate to the season, and taking pride in their work.

Grocery store at Gottingen and Kaye

In addition to the explosion artefacts, there are monuments, added after the church was built in the early fifties, when former members of St. Joseph's Church had settled in this area and become members. One, with a statue of the Virgin Mary, presented by Margaret Walsh in 1954, is in memory of her husband and daughter, killed in the explosion.

Monument at St. Stephen's Park

As St. Stephen's lies almost equidistant from Bedford Basin and the Narrows, another appropriately commemorates the troopships that left from the basin in two world wars, as well as the tragedy of the explosion. An engraving of *Imo* and *Mont Blanc* decorates this stone.

Not far away, on Lady Hammond Road, near the juncture with Robie, is the fire station and the firefighters' memorial. Nine firefighters, including the chief and his deputy, having almost reached *Mont Blanc* to try to extinguish the fire on board, were killed on duty. Their new, modern fire engine, nicknamed Patricia, was very badly damaged and the fire chief's vehicle was wrecked.

St. Stephen's Church

The firefighters' memorial

Patricia and its crew before the explosion

Patricia after the explosion

Fairview Cemetery

Further up Lady Hammond Road towards Bedford Basin, near the juncture with Windsor Street, lies Fairview Cemetery, where there is a memorial to the unidentified dead. As over 150 bodies were buried unidentified, these monuments are very meaningful. If any indication of religious affiliation could be found, the body was buried in the appropriate cemetery.

Memorial to the unidentified dead, Fairview Cemetery

Many victims' graves can also be found. One stone commemorates the forty-five members of *Curaca*'s crew who lost their lives. This freighter, owned by a subsidiary of the Grace Line, with London as home port, bore the full brunt of the explosion and did not come to rest until, seriously damaged, it reached Tufts Cove. The captain survived. "A finer and more good natured body of men never trod the deck of a ship," he said as he deplored the terrible loss, which included the bright junior wireless operator, who had just attained his fourteenth birthday and was a great favourite among the men. Captain Peck had the unpleasant task of identifying the bodies that were recovered. The crew included men from different parts of the world. The horsemen were listed as originally coming from Malta, the two cooks were Chinese. Most of the crew was British. Five of them came from Barra, a little island off the west coast of Scotland. To lose five young men all at once was a severe blow in such a small community. A group of visitors from Barra, including relatives of the men who were lost, will visit Nova Scotia in autumn 2006, and hope to have a memorial service for them, a Roman Catholic service, in Gaelic, with a piper to play a lament.

S.S. Curaca

Gravestone commemorating Curaca's *crew*

Monument to the Unidentified Dead, Bayers Road

Bayers Road Monument

On Bayers Road, not too far away, is a patch of fenced grassy ground. A second monument to the unidentified dead stands near the road. This area of over an acre belongs to and is maintained by Fairview Cemetery. A few burials took place until about fifteen years ago, and some explosion victims, mainly the unidentified dead, were interred there.

In January 1921 the local newspaper noted that plans had been made to improve conditions of the graves of the unidentified victims of the explosion in the part of Bayers Road given over to the city for the burial of the poor: "It is hoped in time to make these graves have the same appearance as those of *Titanic* victims which are a credit to Fairview Cemetery." The good intentions were not carried out, for unknown reasons. The wooden crosses that marked the graves have long since disappeared.

Scouts take part in a wreath-laying ceremony at the Bayers Road monument

West from Bayers Road is Ashburn Avenue. Calvin Presbyterian Church is located here, and outside is a piece of *Mont Blanc*'s anchor shaft, close to where it landed. This area was still largely undeveloped at the time of the explosion.

Piece of anchor shaft at Calvin Presbyterian Church

Mount Olivet Cemetery

At the end of Ashburn Avenue, bordering on Mumford Road and Dutch Village Road, is Mount Olivet Cemetery. Here are the graves of many Catholic victims of the explosion, including some of entire families. The monument to the unidentified Catholic dead, a different shape from the other two, stands at the Olivet Street end, with stones commemorating four crewmembers of HMS *Highflyer* nearby. The cemetery also contains the grave of Captain Michael Maltus of the fire department, who was killed on duty, and the Griswold memorial, which lists the names of sixteen family members killed in the blast.

Mount Olivet Cemetery monument

Not far away, just off Barrington Street near the MacKay Bridge and overlooking the Bedford Basin, is another reminder of the explosion: Mont Blanc Terrace is part of a newly developed area.

Regatta Point (anchor shaft)

At Regatta Point, on the Northwest Arm, is mounted a large piece of anchor shaft not far from where it came to rest after its flight from the shipwreck of *Mont Blanc*.

The Regatta Point anchor shaft in 1918

The anchor shaft in 2005

Dominion Exhibition Grounds

Returning to the city, at the corner of Windsor and Young streets, the large building and parking lots of the Halifax Forum occupy the site of the former Dominion Exhibition Building and the Provincial Exhibition grounds. In December 1917 it held a show of Christmas gifts. The explosion put an end to that. Fortunately it was closed to the public at that time of the morning, but the body of one of the caretakers lay buried there for over a year and a half, its discovery in the summer of 1919 making him the last victim to be found.

In its grounds workmen constructed forty temporary two-storey buildings containing 320 apartments, which were ready for occupation by mid-March 1918. Known as the Governor McCall Apartments, to honour the governor of Massachusetts, they were in five avenues: Endicott, Maine, Massachusetts, Rhode Island, and Fredericton, the names

The Dominion Exhibition grounds, pre-1917

The Exhibition grounds after the explosion

expressing gratitude to places that had sent assistance to Halifax. They held approximately 2200 people. With voluntary help and funds from different organizations, playing fields and the first community centre in Halifax were added, both much needed by people who no longer had access to their familiar places to play or to socialize.

Prior to the explosion, a great deal of a family's social life revolved round the church or school. Living together in temporary housing, with a community centre for everyone, led to the intermingling of religious groups and perhaps contributed to the secularization of social life and personal relations.

The Governor McCall Apartments

The grounds today, featuring the Halifax Forum

Wellington Barracks

From the Forum, Young Street leads past the Hydrostone Market to Gottingen Street. Nearby is the block now occupied by the Royal Canadian Regiment. In 1917 it held the military buildings of Wellington Barracks. One of these was a large, well-stocked magazine with a furnace nearby. After the explosion, live coals escaped from the furnace. Lieutenant MacLennan seized a fire extinguisher, fearful that the flames might reach the magazine and cause enormous damage. He succeeded, but the smoke that rose caused panic and rumours of a second explosion. People were ordered to go to high ground for safety. Rescue operations were impeded, and the general confusion did a great deal of harm. It was some time before the alarm subsided.

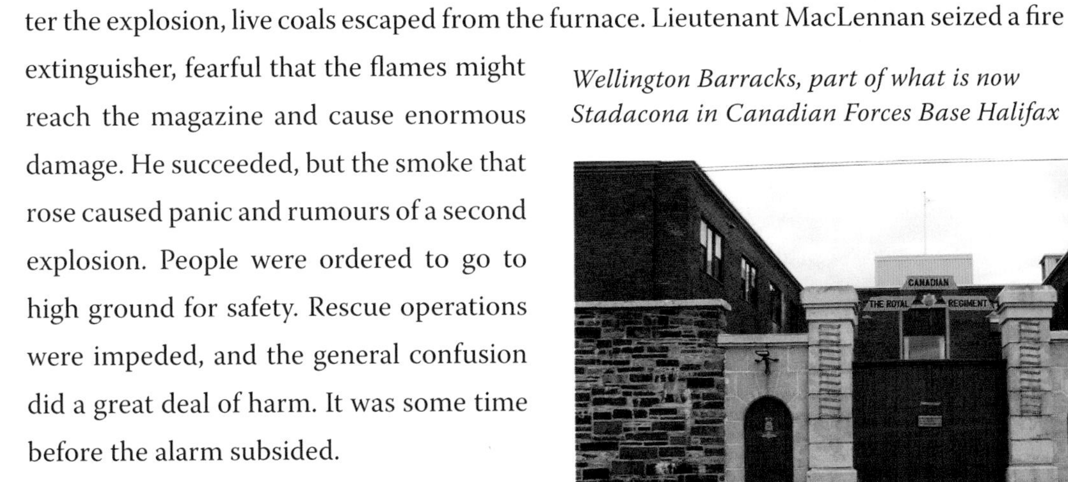

Wellington Barracks, part of what is now Stadacona in Canadian Forces Base Halifax

The Maritime Command Museum, with forecourt

Nearby stands the fine stone Georgian building of the Maritime Command Museum, formerly Admiralty House, completed in 1819 to provide a suitable residence for the Royal Navy's admiral of the North American Station. It has given hospitality to many distinguished visitors over the years, including royal guests. Invitations to receptions, balls, garden parties, and dinners there were eagerly sought. After the departure of the British naval staff in 1905, its use changed and eventually it became a naval hospital. It was damaged in the explosion and its patients were transferred to another hospital. A passing sailor extinguished a fire in the building. Recent roof work has revealed repairs that seem to have been hastily made in 1917. After these repairs were completed, the building was occupied by the Massachusetts-Halifax Relief Committee and the Massachusetts Health Clinic until 1924. In 1974 the building became a museum. The exhibits include a display and documents dealing with the navy's connections with the Halifax Explosion. It is a National Historic Site.

North Street Station

At the foot of North Street, just downhill from Gottingen, stood North Street Station, which marked the southern boundary of the complete devastation. Its glass roof was destroyed and some sixty employees died. The station and the nearby Prince Edward Hotel were given hasty repairs and put back into use again. The construction of the new South Street Station—which was reached through new railway cuts—was sufficiently advanced in 1918 that some of the facilities could be used, especially for the large returning troopships after the end of the war. By the end of 1918, most of the work was completed and

North Street Station

North Street Station after the explosion

Modern-day site of North Street Station

North Street Station hardly used. In June 1921 this grand station, seriously damaged by an accident, was demolished.

Until work began on the Angus L. Macdonald bridge, which opened in 1955, Canadian Meat Packers Ltd. occupied much of the land where the station had once stood.

Kirk and Daughters/Halifax North Memorial Library

Continuing south on Gottingen, just past Prince William Street, comes the Halifax North Memorial Library. In 1917, this was a vibrant part of Gottingen Street. On the block between Prince William and Gerrish streets, the row of buildings, not all of the same height, contained two boot and shoe repairers, a furniture dealer, a butcher, a public market, two home bakeries, two fruit and confectionery shops, and a druggist. Private homes, most of them occupied by the business owners, were on the upper storeys, or between the stores.

Kirk and Daughters Jewellery Store

This Jordi Bonet sculpture once stood outside the Halifax North Memorial Library

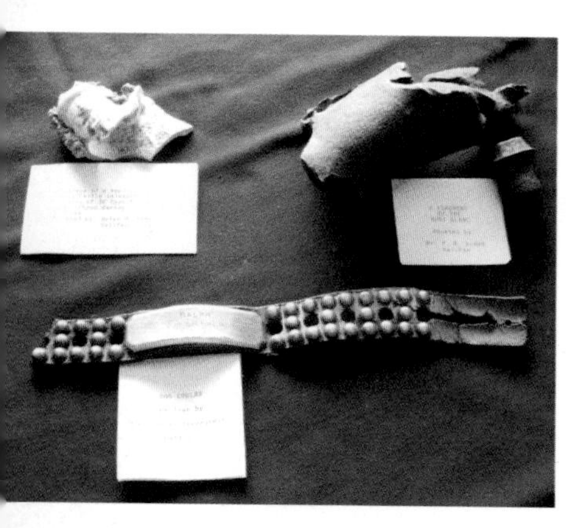

Relics of the explosion, now moved to the Maritime Museum of the Atlantic

Although outside the completely devastated area, there was considerable explosion damage, with shattered windows and roofs caving in.

Kirk and Daughters Jewellery Store stood nearly opposite where the library is now. It is typical of a store with a dwelling on the upper floor.

In July 1966 a headline in the *Mail Star* proclaimed, "Library Seeking Explosion Relics." They had located a piece of *Mont Blanc*'s anchor, which was used in the Jordi Bonet sculpture already unveiled and standing in front of the new building. The building was designed by Keith Graham and Associates and J. D. Solomon and Associates, and was due to be officially opened on October 24 as a memorial to those who lost their lives in the explosion. The Halifax Relief Commission contributed $100,000 to the project, not quite one-sixth of the total cost.

A few relics were donated: two pieces of metal from the ship, a piece of broken pottery, and part of a dog collar. The collar's brass name tag reads:

RALPH
CAPT. H. FROM
S.S. IMO

It was brought by someone who said she had received it from a collector of explosion items, but was not sure of Ralph's fate. A newspaper reported that the dog would not allow strangers to enter his master's cabin on the ship. His loyalty sealed his fate. He was shot so that searching could continue. Some animals were more fortunate than Ralph. The Nova Scotia Society for the Prevention of Cruelty dealt with children as well as animals in 1917, and tried to find homes for animals that had been affected. The Massachusetts SPCA sent workers and help. Domestic animals, like horses and cows, were cared for, and some pets were given new homes.

The explosion relics and a display of photographs can be viewed in the library. Jordi Bonet's sculpture, which originally stood outside the library, has been removed, and a competition for a new one is planned. Minor changes have been made to the building to enlarge the library.

Armouries

The Armouries, built at the end of the nineteenth century as the militia headquarters, and featuring a spacious interior, made a suitable storage place for relief supplies, mainly food at first. The *Montreal Standard* described children picking up food there as "being in the bread line." The building has not changed greatly over the years.

The Armouries in 1917

The Armouries today

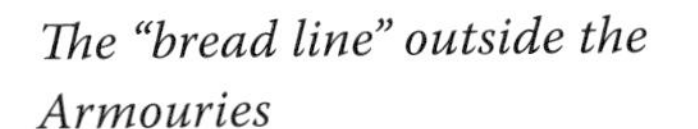

The "bread line" outside the Armouries

Tents on the Commons

The Commons today, with Citadel Hill in the background

Commons

Across from the Armouries lie the Halifax Commons. All early towns and villages in Britain were granted a piece of land for communal grazing and for special activities. This custom continued in British colonies.

By evening on December 6, military tents and a hospital had been erected on the Commons. People were reluctant to use them. Their seemingly safe homes had been destroyed and burnt. Tents were just too flimsy.

Later, in early January 1918, troops began building temporary accommodation for one thousand of the homeless, who began moving there in mid-February.

Chebucto Road School

Across the Commons, on Chebucto Road, Chebucto Road School (now the Maritime Conservatory of Music) witnessed many tragic scenes. After hasty repairs by a company of Royal Engineers, its basement became the official mor-

Chebucto Road School

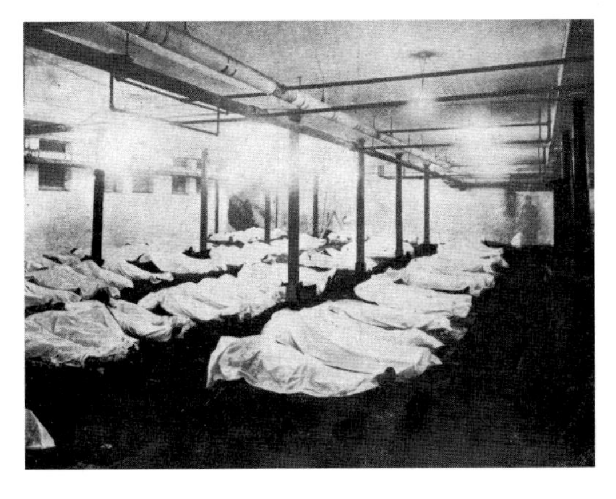

Mortuary at Chebucto Road School

tuary, the upper floors the offices—both, with an incredible effort, opened on December 7. In charge of the mortuary committee was Arthur Barnstead, secretary of industries and immigration for the provincial government. His father's experience with *Titanic* victims just over five years previously must have been partly responsible for the efficiency, as a similar system had been used. Belongings found on bodies and objects lying nearby were placed in linen drawstring bags, and any information that would help in identification was noted. In some cases little was left. "Badly burnt remains of one or more bodies" was sometimes all that could be said. Survivors came to try to find lost family members.

On December 17, 1917, two funeral services (one Roman Catholic, one Protestant) for the unidentified dead, took place in the schoolyard. Most of the bodies were considered unidentifiable, but any sign of

Wallace Baker's family lived on Hurd Lane, not far from the North Common. On the evening of December 5, at a prayer meeting at their house, the group's closing hymn was "Over the Dead-Line." One line in the last verse seemed ominous in retrospect: "And leave thy sad soul in the blast."

The next morning, suddenly, the windows crashed, and the plaster was blown off the walls and ceilings. When Wallace's mother had reassured herself that the four children were not badly hurt, she took them outside. Hurd Lane was "like an obstacle course."

They were ordered to go to Citadel Hill, as the magazine at Wellington Barracks was on fire and a second explosion was feared. There the children were told to go into a trench, where they would be safer.

In the evening Wallace went with his mother to the Commons. He remembers seeing row upon row of benches, covered by white sheets. His mother did what others were doing, lifting corners of the covers to see if she could recognize any members of her prayer group. Nurses and doctors congregated near Cogswell Street and North Park Street. The long flowing headgear of the nurses made a vivid impression on young Wallace.

The following day, they crossed the harbour on the ferry, which had not stopped its service, and took the train to Musquodoboit, the weather worsening as the day went on. They arrived at a relative's house in East Jeddore in deep snow.

Mr. Baker, who had been discharged from the army when war ended in 1918, managed to rent an apartment on the Commons in "a long, barrack-like building covered with tarpaper, held on by one and a half tin discs, with tarpaper nailed through the centre." Theirs was a four-room apartment. The rent was eleven dollars per month. "Father paid me one cent to catch a hundred cockroaches in a tin can, but he finally reneged when there was no end," Wallace remembers.

Public funeral service, December 17, 1917

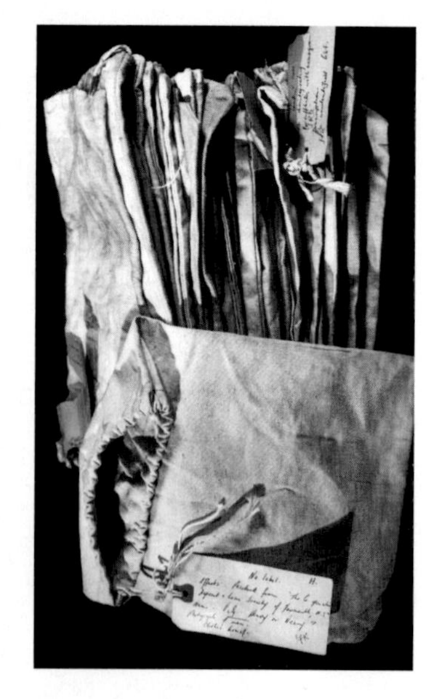

Bags retrieved from the mortuary

religious affiliation was noted. Then came two funeral processions, one to Mount Olivet Cemetery, one to Fairview. Crowds of people attended the ceremonies. These might be the only obsequies for lost relatives. By this time, chances of finding more survivors had grown very slim.

After the mortuary closed in late January 1918, the boxes containing bags of unclaimed effects were stored in the basement of Province House on Granville Street, where Arthur Barnstead could readily make them available to relatives who might come forward in the future. It was assumed, as years went by, that these were the belongings of unidentified victims, but this was not always the case. When they were removed in late November 1981, names, addresses, and descriptions were found on some of the labels. There were letters in a few bags, although not all were ascribed to the right person. The bags and belongings were catalogued, and are now in the Maritime Museum of the Atlantic, where some of them are on view in an exhibit called "Halifax Wrecked."

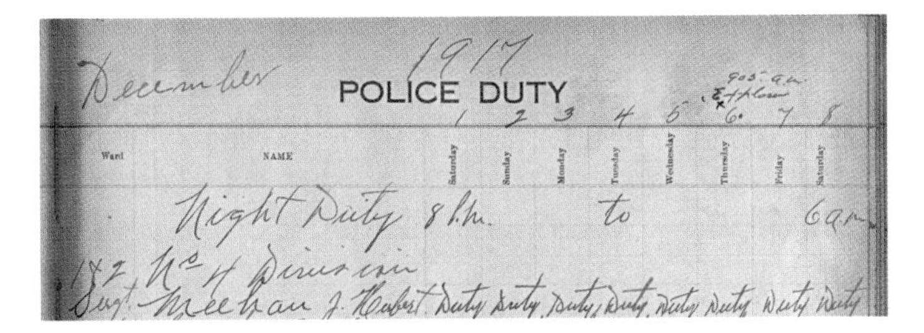
December 1917

POLICE DUTY

Ward	NAME	Saturday	Sunday	Monday	Tuesday	Wednesday	Thursday	Friday	Saturday
	Night Duty 8 P.M. to 6 a.m.								

Police duty time sheet for Thursday, December 6, 1917

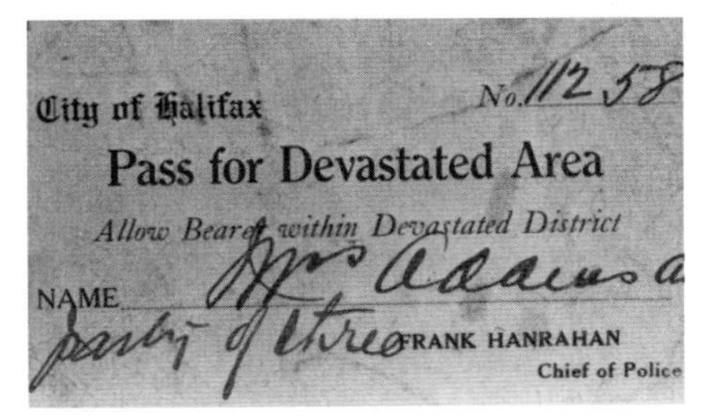
City of Halifax No. 11258

Pass for Devastated Area

Allow Bearer within Devastated District

NAME Mrs Adams

party of three

FRANK HANRAHAN
Chief of Police

A pass granting access to devastated areas

Grand Parade

The clock on the north side of the tower of City Hall, on Grand Parade, in the centre of the city, stopped at the time of the explosion, seconds before 9:05 AM. It was decided that this fateful time should remain permanently displayed. In City Hall, before noon on the day of the explosion, a meeting of city councillors, officials, and other concerned citizens was quickly held, and the basis for relief committees established. Because of their fast decision making, organized relief began early on the afternoon of December 6. City Hall offices became the centre for home relief.

Chief of Police Hanrahan was present at the meeting. With military help, he took charge of the devastated area. It was patrolled night and day. Looting was prevented. Apart from officials, all others required a pass signed by the police chief to enter the devastated area.

Across the Grand Parade, one of the windows in St. Paul's Church shows the outline of a human figure. Legend has it that this was a curate who was hurled by the blast. A fragment of metal from *Mont Blanc* remains where it landed, protruding from the wall of the porch.

The City Hall clock, showing the time of the explosion

St. Paul's Church window

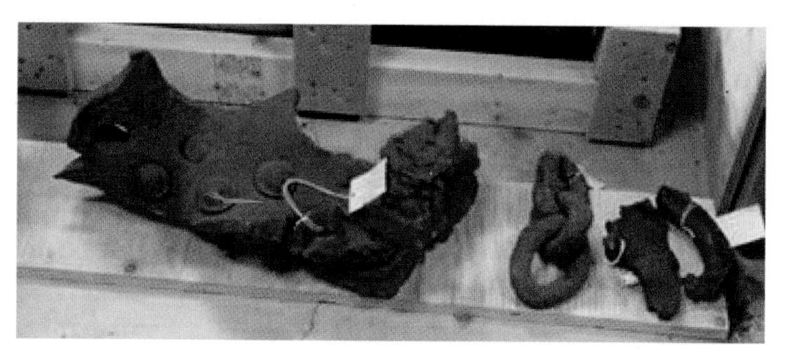

Twisted metal from the Mont Blanc

Maritime Museum of the Atlantic

On Lower Water Street, on the harbour, stands the Maritime Museum of the Atlantic. Part of its structure was an early-nineteenth-century brewery. Inside is "Halifax Wrecked," an explosion-related exhibit, containing photographs, mortuary artefacts, victims' and survivors' accounts, and the Halifax Explosion Memorial Book, a list of those killed in the explosion, with addresses and other details where available.

Many twisted pieces of the *Mont Blanc* are in the museum's collection. They demonstrate the magnitude of the force that shattered the thick metal, causing a shower of the heavy chunks of metal reaching as far as four kilometres from the centre of the explosion. Some were found dug into the ground, others damaged roofs, and for years afterward they were being discovered in gardens and building sites.

Maritime Museum of the Atlantic

Camp Hill Hospital

Every hospital in the city quickly became crowded. Large buildings like schools, halls, and theatres were put to emergency use as shelters or distribution centres. Camp Hill, a military hospital, was newly completed, and a number of military patients—some wounded overseas, some convalescent—had been admitted and treated there. It was, however, not yet fully equipped. Nevertheless, its situation near the Commons brought an influx of explosion victims, causing extreme overcrowding. It contained 280 beds, but an estimated 1,400 injured were admitted on December 6.

Camp Hill Hospital in 1917

The entrance became blocked with vehicles of every description, including wheelbarrows and baby carriages. Recovering military patients were turned out of their beds to make way for the seriously injured. Soon every available space on the floor, in the offices, and in the corridors was taken up with blackened victims, some bleeding, some in shock, some unconscious, some already dead. Tales of horror abounded.

Camp Hill today

Stocks of anaesthetics were insufficient. Some operations were performed fast, while the patients were still unconscious. Volunteers came, one as young as sixteen. Every trained doctor in the city was occupied with emergencies, but as soon as possible, a few came to Camp Hill, bringing their gear. Medical workers from outside the city arrived late that morning and all brought as many useful supplies as they could quickly assemble. It was days before all but the most urgent cases could be treated.

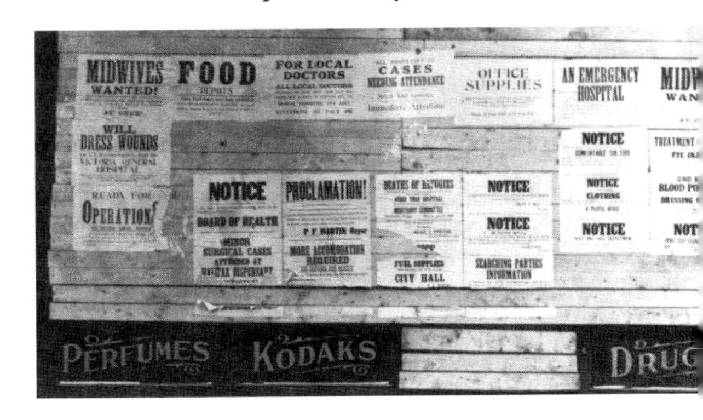

A sign on Barrington Street to attract passers-by

A sign pasted on a wall on Barrington Street gave information and showed that there was a need for help. People reading it would realize that their skills were useful, and would volunteer.

Saint Mary's College Hospital

Saint Mary's College Hospital

With tarpaper over their shattered windows, and camp beds or mattresses to accommodate the enormous need, practically every large building was used as a hospital or shelter, or as a distribution centre for food, clothing, furniture, and other necessities. Education came to a standstill, as universities, colleges, and schools, often with a large red cross near the door, were needed for many special uses.

Halifax Ladies' College, now on Oxford Street and called Armbrae Academy, was then at the corner of Harvey and Barrington streets, on what had been Pleasant Street until earlier that year. It became Maine Military Hospital. St. Mary's College Hospital on Windsor Street, eventually to become St. Mary's University in a new location, was also staffed largely by the military. It treated many eye injuries.

The YMCA building on Barrington Street

YMCA Building

The YMCA on Barrington Street, now the Pacific Building, was one of the early first aid stations. Soon it fulfilled various functions, with dressing stations, a temporary hospital, and also a very welcome soup kitchen run by volunteers. Many babies were taken to the temporary hospital there. It was difficult to be absolutely certain of identification in many cases, especially if the mother had been killed or the father was in the armed services overseas.

Babies at the YMCA hospital.

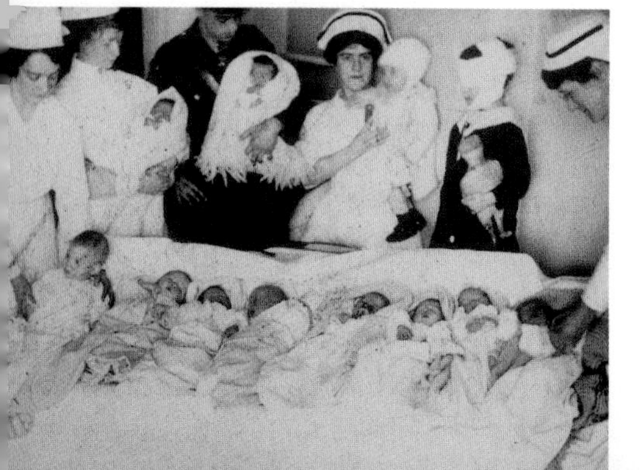

Every military and private hospital quickly became overcrowded. Mattresses on the floor held the extra casualties.

Theatres, halls, and clubs were soon bustling with activity as medical and relief workers poured into the city, bringing much needed supplies. Naval ships in the harbour, with their infirmaries, also provided care. Large buildings, like church halls and Salvation Army posts, became shelters for the homeless. The Academy of Music on Barrington and the Knights of Columbus Hall on Hollis made suitable places of refuge.

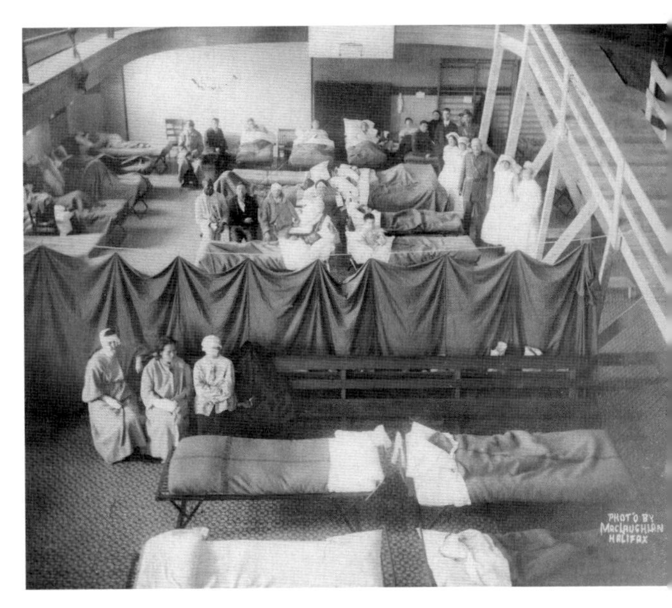

Interior of a temporary hospital

Rockhead Prison

Rockhead Prison, closer to the site of the explosion, was soon filled with the homeless, many from Grove Presbyterian Church, where the prison governor was a parishioner. It was said that some of the prisoners, who were working in the garden at the time of the explosion, had taken advantage of the broken walls and made their escape.

Rockhead Prison

Nova Scotia Technical College

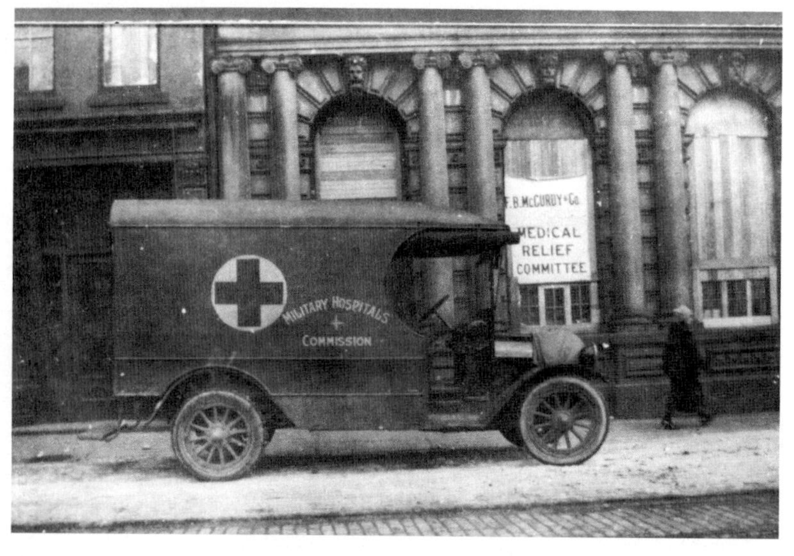

The F. B. McCurdy Building on Hollis Street housed the Medical Relief Committee

Nova Scotia Technical College

The Nova Scotia Technical College on Spring Garden Road became the Central Medical Supply Depot. It was a vital part of the relief effort, with constant comings and goings of every type of vehicle seeking the supplies that were lacking, especially in temporary hospitals. The college had been founded in 1909 as part of an effort to improve the level of industrial education in Nova Scotia. It is now a part of Dalhousie University.

The first relief committees were formed on December 6, and the others over the next few days as requirements became obvious. There were committees for managing reconstruction, transportation, food, clothing, fuel, rehabilitation, medical relief, medical supply, emergency shelter, supply, finance, mortuary, information, registration, employment, animals, and children. There was also an overall executive committee.

Thus, survivors searching for families often had to cover many sites. This made the registration committee, one of the earliest to be formed, invaluable. The City Club on Barrington Street fulfilled several functions. Registration, fuel, and emergency shelter were all organized in the building.

On the same side of Barrington Street, from Spring Garden Road to Sackville Street, were the large buildings of St. Mary's Convent, St. Mary's Parish Hall, Halifax Infirmary, St. Mary's Hall, the City Club, and the Church of England Institute. All were used as shelters or hospitals. The facades of some of the buildings that were there in 1917 can still be seen, but their uses have changed.

Most restaurants distributed food, while the Green Lantern on Barrington Street specialised in clothing and footwear. One survivor remembered with great affection a beautiful green coat she obtained there. This restaurant stood on Barrington Street just to the north of the Roy Building, which remains but with completely different tenants from those in 1917.

It was from books like the one to the right, published soon after the explosion, that we know as much as we do about that day in December 1917. Lieutenant Colonel F. McKelvey Bell was involved in rescue work and was so badly affected by the experience that he took considerable time off afterward, when he wrote the illustrated book pictured here.

RELIEF ORDER

Case No. 2155 In favor of Order No.

Name Robert Campbell

Address 134 Edward Street

To Clothing Depot (Station or Dealer) Green Lantern Date Dec. 29, 19

You are authorized to deliver to the above named person, or to the above address (BUT TO NO OTHER ADDRESS, except upon the request of the Rehabilitation Committee), the following articles.

LADIES' CLOTHING:

one black dress, size 36" (for elderly woman)

three pairs stockings, size 10.

one pair gloves, 6½

one muffler (furs, etc. have been lost)

GIRL'S CLOTHING:

(Ages 10) (and 11) 2 hats, (or caps) 2 warm dresses, 2 pairs mittens

BOY'S CLOTHING:

Age 14 1 cap, 1 suit clothes (knee pants) 2 night shirts, 2

socks, 1 suit underwear, 1 pr. mittens

MAN'S CLOTHING:

1 suit clothes, 38", 1 suit underwear, 38", 1 pr. glo

2 night shirts, 3 prs. socks, 2 top shirts, 15½", 1 rain c

NOTE—To prevent errors, a description of these goods should be required of the applicant before delivery.

Authorized by Awards Committee, [Insert date of decision] or

Received the above goods Shipped by

An order for clothing

One of several books about the explosion published soon after December 1917

Dartmouth

Dartmouth was spared the total destruction experienced in Halifax, in part because its North End was less developed and less populated than that of Halifax. From its beginnings, Dartmouth's waterfront had lent itself to industries, but gradually development had pushed away from the shore as newer enterprises arrived and the population expanded. Among the town's most obvious physical features, in addition to its fine waterfront, were its numerous lakes and many hills. People living in the town took the hills for granted, and since there was no public transportation, walking was the accepted way to get to work or school. The downtown area was heavily populated in 1917, with some families living in flats over their stores. On Portland, Ochterloney, and Water streets there were about a dozen grocery stores, several drug stores, clothing stores, stationery and candy stores, and small restaurants. Single-family homes were modest, but there were also some larger ones to accommodate boarders. Apartments were unheard of in those days, but many a widow supplemented her income by taking boarders.

On the hills were many fine estates, taking advantage of the wonderful views of Halifax and the harbour. Some of these had been built by Halifax residents as summer places, but they gradually became year-round homes. These houses had names, but unfortunately many of them have disappeared, such as Sunny Brae, the Octagon House, Maplehurst, Hazelhurst, Beechwood, and the original Brightwood. Still remaining are Mount Amelia, Sunnyside, Lakeside, Edgemere, Stoneyhurst, and Evergreen. The latter is preserved as a historic home and is now in use as the Dartmouth Heritage Museum. All these houses were still standing in 1917.

After the large industries had come to town, streets had been developed and housing built in the North End near the brewery and the ropeworks, and in the South End near the sugar and oil refineries.

Five main roads radiated out from the ferry to Dartmouth's town limits, which were a little over a mile from the ferry. Outside the town limits Pleasant Street led to Woodside, Imperoyal, and Eastern Passage; Portland Street went to Woodlawn and Cole Harbour; Prince Albert Road divided at "Johnny Graham's Corner" (now the Parclo), one branch going to Preston, Chezzetcook, and the Eastern Shore, and the other winding out past the beautiful chain of lakes to Waverley, and thence to Truro and across the province; Water Street, just up from the ferry (now called Alderney Drive) followed the harbour north, changing its name to Windmill Road, at the bottom of the first hill, known as Synott's Hill for a family who had lived there. Windmill Road led eventually to Bedford but before that it passed through Tufts Cove, which is a focal point in this account of the Halifax Harbour Explosion. All roads leading out of Dartmouth, and indeed most of them within the town limits, were unpaved in 1917.

Two railway bridges in the late 1800s had connected Dartmouth and Halifax, but both ended in disaster. However, Dartmouth had been given a rail link to the main Intercolonial Railway from Windsor Junction to Meagher's Grant, just past Musquodoboit Harbour. The track snaked along the shoreline passing businesses and their wharves on the harbour, a valuable addition for transportation to the rest of the province and the rest of Canada.

Dartmouth was often considered a bedroom town for Halifax, linked as the two were by an excellent ferry service, run by the Dartmouth Ferry Commission. Although employment within the town was at an all-time high, there was still a need for people to commute daily to Halifax. High school students were given a free pass on the ferry to attend the Halifax County Academy at the corner of Sackville and Brunswick streets, in downtown Halifax. Many people worked in Halifax as bank clerks, teachers, doctors, nurses, lawyers, mechanics—at any number of jobs.

The ferry Halifax

Tufts Cove
DARTMOUTH
HALIFAX
Halifax Harbour
Brightwood Golf and Country Club
Little Albro Lake
Angus L. MacDonald Bridge
Windmill Rd
Victoria Rd
Wyse Rd
Pinecrest Dr
Albro Lake Rd
Woodland Ave
Nivens Ave
Hester St
Green Rd
Nantucket Ave
Fairbanks St
Shore Rd
Barrington St
Devonshire Ave
Young St
Gottingen St
Albert St
Union St
Needham St
Kaye St
Russell St
Richmond St
Veith St
Hanover St
Sullivan St
Isleville St
Connor Ln
Nookta Ave
Fernhill Dr
Ferguson Rd
Tidewater Ln
Stone Ave
Wournell Dr
Hitchie Rd
Parkstone Rd
Trinity Ave
Springhill Rd
Yorkshire Ave
Kenwood Dr
Bethel Ave
Alfred St
Elwood Dr
Gibson St
Lovett St
Pinewood Dr
Sunnydale Ave
Middle St
India St
Catherine St
Courtney Rd
Farrell St
Lahey Rd
Clarence St
Wallace St
Howe St
Bedford St
Stairs St
Haig St
Elmwood Ave
Mitchell St
Floral Ave
Rosedale Dr
Henry St
Grove St
Fraser St
Jamieson St
Brookside Ave
Dillman Pl
Pelzant St
George St
John St
Bligh St
Dawson St
Faulkner St
Dickson St
Williams St
Lyle St
MacDonald Bridge
Best St
Mott St
Hare Ln
Chappell St
Richmond St
Russell St
Symonds St
Chapman St
Slayter St
Sheridan St
Moira St
Pinehill Rd
Jackson Rd
Robert Burns Dr
Primrose St
Burke St
Brule St
Cedar Crt
Leaman Dr
Ernest Ave
Emmanuel Dr
Beldina Dr
Limardo Dr
Wallingham St
Laurier St
Ryland Ave
Charles St
Frederick St
Lorraine St
Birchwood Terr
Clarke St
Vanessa Dr
Frances St
Eastbrook Ave
Westbrook Ave
Graham St
Murray St
Boland Rd
Cairn St
Nova Crt
Chabucto Ln
Scotia Crt
Bras Dor Ln
Canso Ln
Fundy Ln
Cherry Dr
Garden Dr
Shamrock Dr
Thistle St
2
3
4
5
6
7
8
9
10
11
12
13
14
15
16
17
18
19
20
21
22
28
32
42

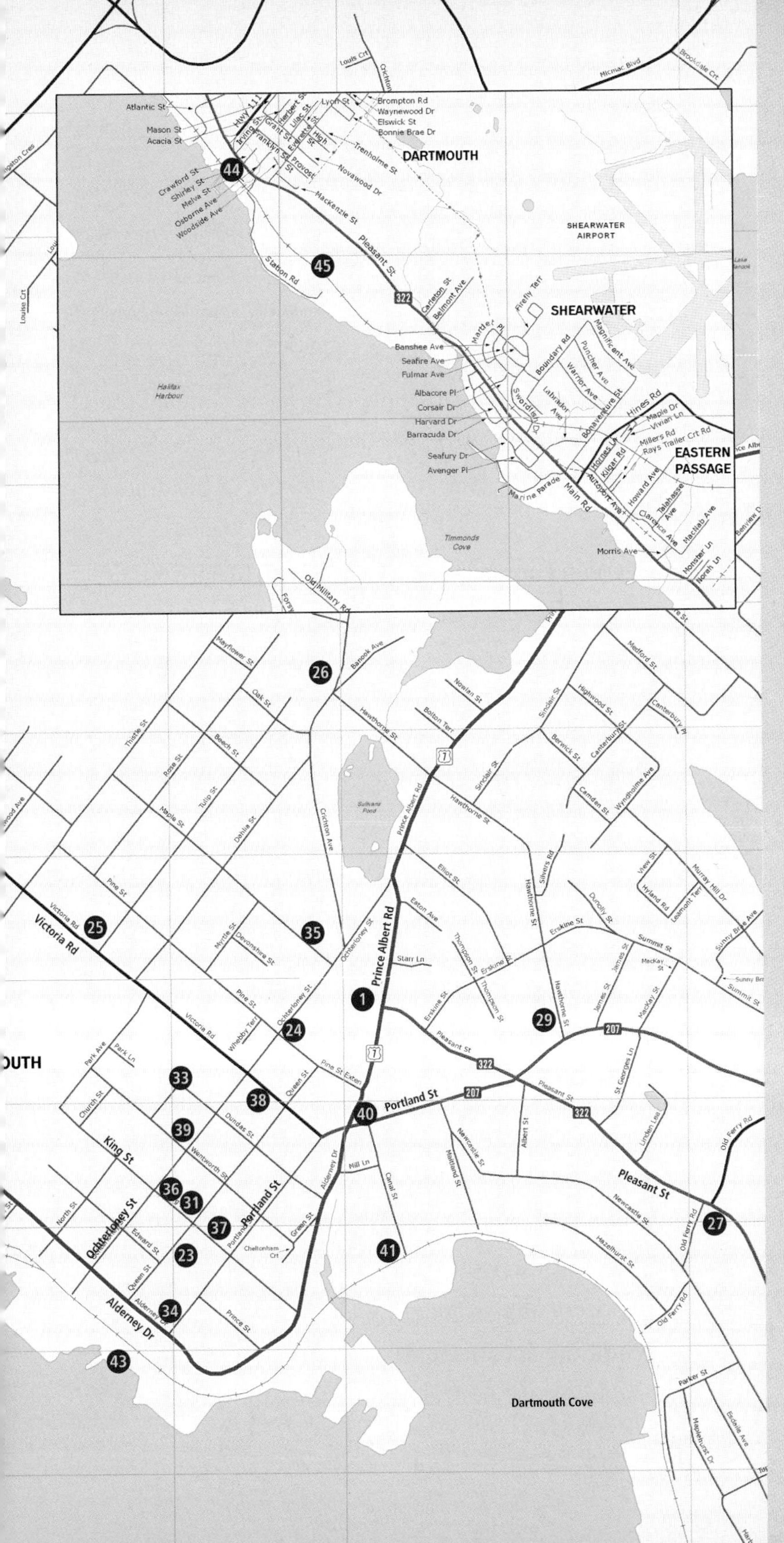

1 Starr Manufacturing
2 Tufts Cove
3 Turtle Grove
4 Turtle Grove School
5 Dumaresq house
6 Rice house
7 Tufts Cove School
8 Williston Steel Foundry
9 North ferry landing
10 French Cable Wharf and Building
11 Oland Brewery ruins
12 Crathorne house and mill
13 *Imo* beaching site
14 Pettipas house
15 Tufts Cove Cemetery
16 Dartmouth Ropewalk Company
17 Seven Sisters
18 Emmanuel Church
19 Stairs Church (1917)
20 Stairs Church (2006)
21 Bethel Baptist mission church
22 Mont Blanc Memorial Park
23 Dr. Burris's house and office
24 Greenvale School
25 Fairview
26 Edgemere
27 Beechwood
28 Dartmouth rink and range light
29 Hawthorne School
30 First Park School
31 Central School
32 Victoria School
33 Christ Church Hall
34 Sterns Corner
35 St. Peter's Church
36 Grace Church
37 Old Baptist Church
38 New Baptist Church
39 Christ Church
40 Church of St. James
41 Rolling Mill
42 Victoria Park
43 Modern Dartmouth ferry terminal
44 Acadia Sugar Refinery
45 Imperial Oil

On the cool, sunny morning of December 6, 1917, Dartmouthians whose work took them to Halifax each day assembled as usual in the new ferry terminal waiting for the next boat. A crowd had collected at one window to watch the manoeuvring of *Imo* and *Mont Blanc* near the Narrows. It seemed that the ships were about to pass in a rather confined space. Just then the ferry arrived from Halifax, the doors of the terminal opened, and the crowd walked down the ramp to board the boat. Some passengers climbed the companionway for their morning constitutional on the upper deck, while others stayed down below for the warmth and sociability of the cabin. All were unaware of the drama unfolding rapidly at the Narrows.

Soon after, the passengers witnessed a shocking spectacle: the collision, the fire on the old freighter *Mont Blanc*, and the catastrophic explosion.

THE SITES

The explosion would touch Dartmouth first with the landing of *Mont Blanc*'s crew in lifeboats. Because of conflicting stories and court evidence, it is difficult to establish exactly where the two lifeboats landed on the Dartmouth side. In his *Story of Dartmouth,* Dr. John Martin wrote that they landed at Jamieson Street. However, just days after the event, On December 13, 1917, a Wreck Commissioner's Court, presided over by Supreme Court Justice Arthur Drysdale began in the courthouse on Spring Garden Road. Captain Le Medec of *Mont Blanc* gave evidence in court that the boats rowed at an oblique angle and went ashore just north of the French Cable Building, which is somewhat north of Jamieson Street. There, the captain immediately took a head count and ascertained that all forty men had landed. Crewmembers then rushed in all directions to take cover in the woods. There were approximately eighteen to twenty minutes between the time of the collision and the actual explosion. Every man in the two lifeboats while crossing the harbour had been terrified, expecting the explosion at any moment.

Pilot Francis Mackey, who had been in one of *Mont Blanc*'s lifeboats, also testified at the Drysdale Inquiry, saying that the boats landed at "a little jut of land, a ferry landing." This may have been George Holmes's ferry landing at the bottom of Jamieson Street, thus agreeing with Dr. Martin, or it could have been the Duggans' north ferry landing at the foot of Grove Street, close to the French Cable property, but this does not tally with the Captain's statement that the lifeboats landed just north of the French Cable Building. The shoreline has changed greatly since 1917, and there were a number of wharves and little coves at that time that have since disappeared on charts of the harbour.

Possible locations for the landing of Mont Blanc's *lifeboats*

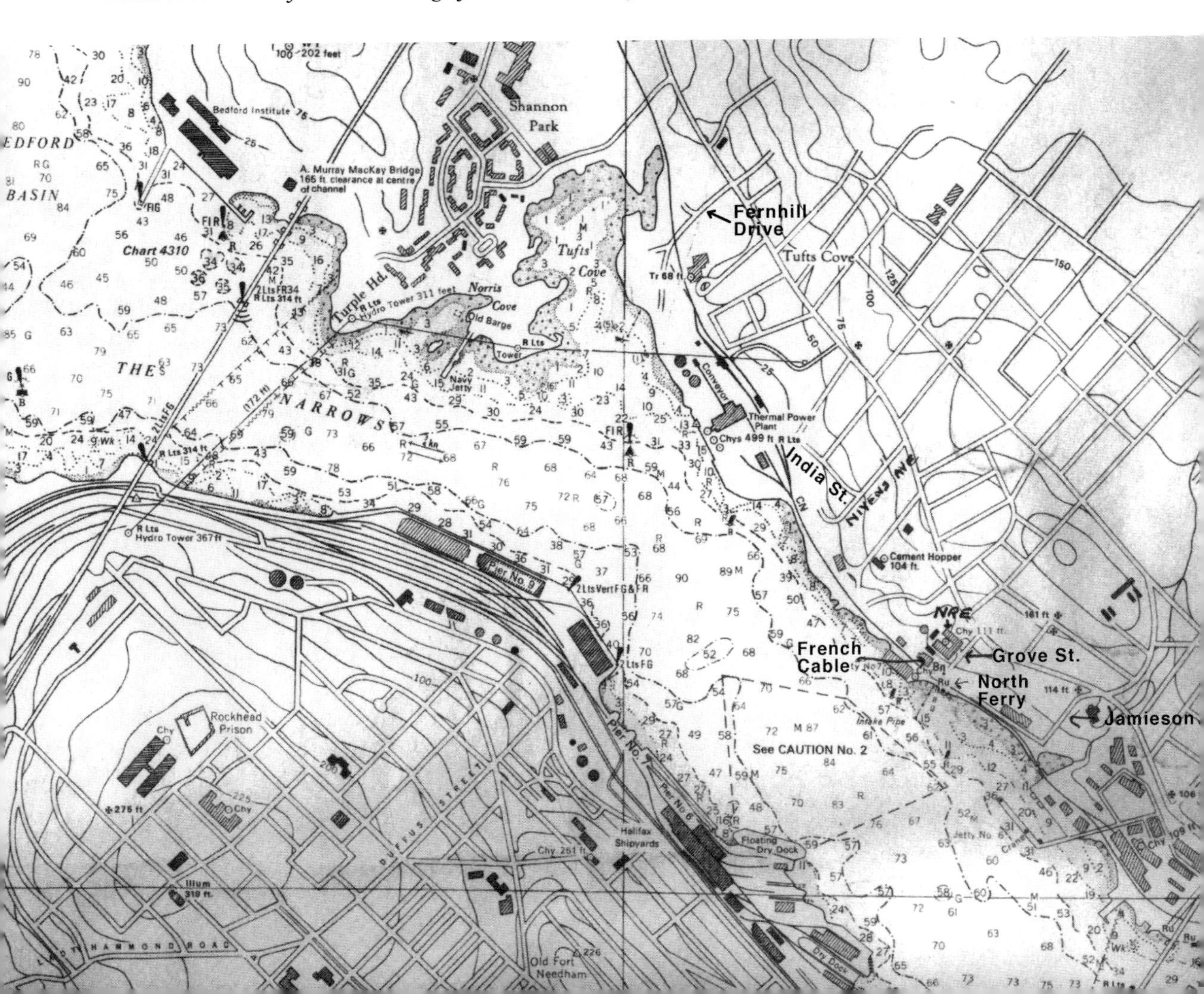

At the inquiry, C. J. Burchell, lawyer for the company that owned *Imo*, questioned Mackey rather mercilessly, asking whether he had considered going to the telephone on the brewery wharf to warn people about the explosion that he knew was about to happen. Mackey replied that it had occurred to him to do this after the explosion, but he could not get anyone on the phone. The cable for the phone system came across the harbour at this location and the connection had been broken by the blast. Surprisingly, after the dreadful panic of the morning, Mackey was able to make his way downtown to the main ferry boat, and crossed over to Halifax. Captain Le Medec was given a drive by one of the volunteers who were taking the injured from the north end to doctors downtown for help.

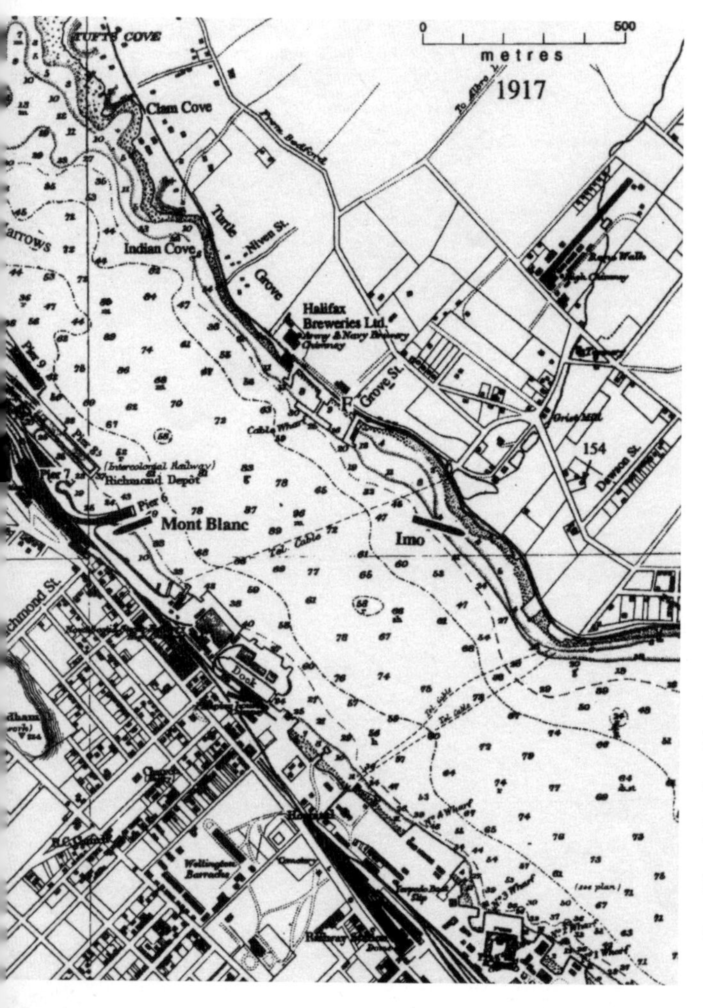

Chart of the shoreline in 1917

Only one member of *Mont Blanc*'s crew was seriously injured: Yves Gueguiner, the gunner. He was hit by shrapnel, and Captain Le Medec told the inquiry he had died from loss of blood. Years later, Lois Richards of the Dartmouth Historical Association interviewed two sisters, Margaret and Mollie Kuhn, who were schoolgirls at the time of the explosion. They told her that they were walking to safety away from the town when they saw a minister, Rev. J. A. MacGlashen, praying over a dying French sailor, who must have been Yves Gueguiner. This adds further confusion to the landing place of the lifeboats, because MacGlashen lived in the new Presbyterian manse next door to Emmanuel Church on the corner of Dawson Street, which is south again of Jamieson Street. The manse was destroyed in the blast, and it was unlikely that MacGlashen would be as far north as the Fernhill Drive neighbourhood. But that poses another question. Would the French sailor have been able to walk the considerable distance to MacGlashen's neighbourhood before he died from loss of blood?

Owing to its larger population, Halifax suffered far more death and destruction than did Dartmouth. But for the people of Tufts Cove, just outside the town limits, and those who lived or worked along the Dartmouth shore of the harbour, the death toll and destruction were proportionately disastrous. The tsunami that resulted from the explosion sent two or three large waves up the low-lying, wooded shores of Dartmouth.

Several accounts were given at the Drysdale Inquiry by people who had withstood the force of the rushing water containing all manner of dangerous debris. One such description was given by George Dixon, a Tufts Cove native and employee of McKean's Ship Building Company, which was located between Indian Cove and Clam Cove. W. K. McKean built schooners and was president of George McKean and Co. Lumber Dealers. Dixon's story results in yet another possible landing place for *Mont Blanc*'s lifeboats.

Lenora Cross was a twenty-six-day-old baby on the day of the explosion, and is still living at the time of this writing. She holds another opinion about the *Mont Blanc* crew's landing place. At the time she was living with her family on a small, unpaved street now called Fernhill Drive. Their house was up a hill above Tufts Cove. Only a few families lived in that location, but word of the fire in the harbour spread quickly and neighbours ran down the hill to the shore for a better look. Mrs. Marsh, mother of Lenora, carried the tiny baby in her arms. She and her neighbours were startled suddenly by lifeboats approaching the shore. The strange men jumped out screaming and gesticulating, urging people to run, but since they were speaking in French their orders were not understood. In desperation one sailor had the clever idea to seize little Lenora from her mother's arms and keep running. Naturally the mother and her neighbours were horrified and raced after the man, perhaps saving their lives. Just then the noise of the earth-shaking explosion of *Mont Blanc* stunned the entire area for miles around. This story from Mrs. Cross is very convincing as to where the crew landed, but she herself is quick to say that because she was such a young baby at the time, she could not swear to it.

Tufts Cove from the top of Fernhill Drive

Lenora Cross in 2005

On the day of the explosion, Dixon watched the unfolding drama from the Dartmouth shore opposite Halifax's Pier 9. He testified in court at the Drysdale Inquiry that he had heard the actual collision of *Imo* and *Mont Blanc.* The force of the ensuing explosion caused Dixon to turn a somersault, and he said a house was blown down in the neighbourhood, while the water was boiling with flying metal. Then he was aware of the tidal wave coming towards him, which rushed up and surrounded the bungalows on the shore. He was questioned by a lawyer, Humphrey Mellish, about one of these cottages owned by architect Walter Busch just a little north of Indian Cove. Dixon replied that the cottage was "where the ferry used to run in summer...there is a cove above...where the ship building plant is, called Clam Cove...where a ferry used to run in the summer time."

The shoreline has changed substantially from that shown on the 1917 chart. Could this ferry landing have been the one referred to by Pilot Francis Mackey as "a little jut of land, a ferry landing, that is where we went"? If so, the story of the baby being grabbed by the French sailor would be plausible, because Fernhill Drive was far closer to this summertime ferry landing than to the Grove Street ferry landing.

Turtle Grove

Turtle Grove

The Turtle Grove school

South of McKean's shipbuilding operation was the Mi'kmaq village of Turtle Grove. In the summer, wigwams were scattered among the evergreens where several families made their homes, an idyllic spot for fishing and for travelling by canoe along the shore. In the winter, a few of the families had simple wooden houses further inland. Family names included Lonecloud, Paul, Prosper, Labrador, Glode, and Nevins. They earned their living by making and selling a great variety of goods and handcrafts, including paddles, oars, hockey sticks, and baskets. The settlement had been in this place for many years, probably before the arrival of Governor Edward Cornwallis in 1749. A few years before the explosion, a dispute about the ownership of the eleven acres that comprised Turtle Grove had been occupying the provincial government and the Department of Indian Affairs. Then, ironically, only one month before the explosion, the government had settled the matter, enabling the families to move to a new reservation at nearby Albro Lake.

It was a terrible misfortune that the move did not happen in time to save the community from the explosion. The fire on the ship attracted the attention of everyone along the shoreline, and the Mi'kmaq were no exception. At least nine of them were killed in Turtle Grove by the explosion, the tidal wave, or the fires in their homes.

Mi'kmaq children attended a school built on land donated by William Nevins, one of the few Mi'kmaq who owned property. On that fateful morning, children were in the school waiting for their teacher, George Richardson, a Halifax man. He, however, was late because he had stopped on the Halifax side to watch the *Mont Blanc* fire. He was instantly killed in the blast, while on the other side of the Narrows his school collapsed, killing some of his pupils and injuring others.

The exact number of Mi'kmaq who lived in the community was not known, so as a result neither was there an exact count of the number of deaths. A few days after the explosion, newspaper accounts listed some of the Turtle Grove residents at shelters at Imperial Oil and at the Nova Scotia Hospital, part of which was used for people injured in the explosion. Nine bodies were recovered from the Mi'kmaq community but more may have died. Except for the Nevins and the Lone Cloud families, those who escaped death in the explosion moved to other reservations in the province or went to live elsewhere with relatives or friends. The new reservation at Albro Lake never materialized.

Today, Nova Scotia Power's thermal plant occupies the space where the Mi'kmaq had their homes. Three huge smoke stacks dominate the Tufts Cove horizon in sharp contrast to the little village shown in old sketches and photos. There is still a road leading from Windmill Road down towards the harbour named Nivens Avenue, and near the end of it India Road branches off to the north, ending at the fenced land of the power corporation. On older maps of the area these two names were printed as "Nevins" and "Indian," which were probably the correct spellings.

William Dumaresq's home

Here on Indian Road occurred one of the worst tragedies for a single family. William Dumaresq's house faced the harbour and the burning ship. Mrs. Dumaresq and her little daughter, Vera, were looking out the window at the fire, and both were blinded as the window shattered. Two younger children in the house later died of their injuries, and William Dumaresq himself was killed at work in the nearby brewery. One son, Lawrence, survived without serious injuries. Vera Dumaresq went on to attend the School for the Blind in Halifax, became an excellent pianist, and taught music after her graduation from the school. But the Dumaresqs' family life was ruined forever.

William Dumaresq's home

Home of Lieutenant Rice

Home of Lieutenant Rice

Nearby on Windmill Road, in Tufts Cove, was the home of Lieutenant Rice, who was stationed with the army in Sydney. His wife had stayed in Dartmouth to care for their small children, and she also boarded three Kuhn sisters from Cole Harbour (previously mentioned in connection with Rev. Mr. MacGlashen), who were attending schools in Halifax and Dartmouth. The two older girls, Mollie and Margaret, were at the Halifax Academy, and when they returned to their boarding house by way of the ferry and a long walk, they found it in ruins, with Clara Rice lying lifeless within. It was a terrible shock for those young girls and also for Lieutenant Rice.

Tufts Cove School

In addition to the school for Mi'kmaq children, at the northeast corner of Albro Lake and Windmill Roads was the Tufts Cove School. Originally this school was built for the Town of Dartmouth in 1891, but in 1908 it had been turned over to the County of Halifax, because it was just outside the town's boundary line. The school was irreparably damaged in the explosion, but luckily, since county schools did not open until nine thirty during the winter months, there had been no children inside at the time of the explosion. Eventually a new school replaced the wrecked one, but it, too, has long since disappeared, and Farrell Hall now occupies the busy intersection.

Tufts Cove School

Williston Steel Foundry

Williston Steel Foundry

Farther south on Windmill Road near Grove Street, the substantial new Williston Steel Foundry had opened for business eighteen months prior to the explosion. However, it was not a financial success so fortunately it, too, was idle on that fateful day, awaiting start-up by new owners. The building was a total wreck, and today even the skeleton of the foundry is no more.

The north ferry terminal, Grove Street

Grove Street had a great deal of foot traffic for many years, because of the north ferry at the bottom of the hill. The ferries landed their passengers across the harbour between the naval dockyard and the Halifax shipyard where steep wooden steps climbed up to Barrington Street. Before the days of cars, buses, or bridges, the ferries were invaluable to people living in north Dartmouth and Tufts Cove whose work took them to Halifax. Several family names are associated with the ownership and operations of the north ferry routes from both Grove Street and Jamieson Street a little further south—Heffler, Keans, Duggan, Mooney, Holmes, and Dauphinee.

The north ferry terminal and ferry boats at the foot of Grove Street

On the morning of the explosion, Charles Duggan tried to use his ferry to rescue passengers from the burning *Mont Blanc*. When he saw that there was no one left on board, and that barrels were exploding on the ship's deck, he wisely turned his ferry away from the scene and headed for Dartmouth. On December 12, 1917, he told the *Daily Echo*:

I was standing in the boat looking backward toward the *Mont Blanc* when she appeared to settle in the water. A lurid yellowish-green spurt of flame rose toward the heavens and drove ahead of it a cloud of smoke which must have risen two hundred feet in the air. Then came the most appalling crash I have ever heard, and my boat went under my feet as if some supernatural power had stolen her from me while I myself was thrown into the harbour.

At the time of the explosion a second licensed north ferry service, operated by George Holmes, was running from the foot of Jamieson Street. Holmes had a close call with death when he was washed ashore in Halifax by the tsunami, landing on a pile of cinders. He was thought to be dead and taken to the morgue, where he was recognized by his sister Emily, an army nurse. Luckily, she heard her brother give a small groan and realized he was in a coma. He was quickly taken to a hospital, where he recovered slowly. His boat had been wrecked, but in any case he had no desire to return to operating a ferry again.

Captain C. Wesley Dauphinee, interviewed in 1978, recounted this story of Charlie Duggan and mentioned the name of the ferry, *Gray Starling*. The ferry was blown out of the water, landing in a north Dartmouth field. This seemed an appropriate name for a boat that flew, and it was so named in a photo included in a book on the history of the Dartmouth–Halifax ferries, *Like a Weaver's Shuttle*, published in 1979. However, in a follow-up interview, Captain Dauphinee said the name of the boat as printed in the book was quite wrong and he could not understand how the mistake had occurred. The correct name, he said, was *Grace Darling* because the ferry had been named for the girl of the famous (and true) legend about a lighthouse keeper's daughter. The girl had helped her father rescue nine survivors of a shipwreck off Britain's Northumbrian coast during a fierce storm. Readers who quickly pronounce the two different names may forgive the author's mistake. *Grace Darling* was repaired and returned to the north ferry route for several years after its flight.

Interior of a ferry

At the time of the explosion, ferry passengers were crowding the rails of the upper deck, or kneeling on the seats in the cabins below looking out the windows. When it came, the explosion was an unbelievable shock. Passengers in the cabin were cut by shattered glass, or knocked unconscious as they were blown backwards, hitting their heads on the upright steam radiators that ran down the length of the cabin.

Three passengers, interviewed by the author in 1978, each had slightly different impressions of their experience. Dorothy MacLennan, a young bank clerk, was on the deck. After the explosion a soldier shepherded passengers to the shelter of the companionway, where they lay down on top of one another in case there was a second blast. Dorothy was unscathed and unaware of any unusual wave motion during the experience. Theresa O'Regan, down in the cabin, on her way to her secretarial job, was badly cut by window glass, but had the impression that the ferry's engines had stopped and then started up again. A third young woman, Hattie Gibson, travelling across with her sister, Marguerite, said that they were both momentarily knocked unconscious when thrown against the cabin's radiators, but in spite of this they felt the ferry sink down and then bob up again as if the harbour's waters had parted.

When the ferry docked on the Halifax side, Dorothy MacLennan made her way up to the Royal Bank where she worked, but all staff members were told to return home. Back on the deck of the ferry, she and other passengers were aghast when they gazed at the north ends of both Halifax and Dartmouth. Buildings were flattened, flames were already licking the piles of collapsed structures and the amount of destruction was utterly incomprehensible.

To the great credit of ferry employees, the boats operated all day long and through the following night, thus aiding in the frantic personal searches for lost relatives, transporting patients to hospitals, and carrying supplies of food, clothing, and medical equipment where they were needed. The staff of the ferry commission were among the many heroes of that dreadful day.

Dorothy MacLennan on the ferry deck

French Cable Wharf

On the north side of Grove Street today is the complex of Defence R and D Canada Atlantic (originally named the Naval Research Establishment, and then renamed Defence Research Establishment Atlantic). Among its other activities related to naval affairs, this institution was heavily involved in the Canadian hydrofoil ship project. Part of the northern end of the establishment includes a handsome grey building close to the railway tracks that run along the shore of the harbour. Architect R. A. Johnson designed the front of the building to face the harbour. Just underneath its slightly overhanging roof, its original name and date of construction stand out: Compagnie Française des Cables Télégraphiques, 1916. The official opening took place in 1917. Somewhat like the Williston Foundry, it was a new construction when assaulted by the explosion, but unlike the foundry it weathered the assault, thanks to its thick reinforced concrete walls. Cable was manufactured inside the building, which also contained the caretaker's residence.

At its equally sturdy wharf, the cable ship *Edouard Jeramec*, under the command of Captain Julien Lemarteleur, was a familiar sight after working at sea attending to the company's Atlantic cables crossing from France. Fortunately, the cable ship had gone to sea the day before the explosion and so escaped damage. The explosion did damage the cable in the harbour, but not as badly as did an earthquake and tsunami off the coast of

The French cable building on the left, with the ruins of a less sturdy building on the right

Compagnie Française des Cables Télégraphiques

Newfoundland in 1929, which broke the transatlantic cables of various companies. The two familiar ships of the Western Union Cable Company, *Lord Kelvin* and *Cyrus Field*, which docked beside the Halifax terminal of the main cross-harbour ferries, helped in the restoration of all cables after that upheaval. In that same year of 1929, the French company was sold to All America Cables.

After the sale of the Compagnie Française des Cables Télégraphiques there was very little activity at the French Cable Wharf, but a caretaker named Felix Claireaux lived with his family on company property, their address designated as 219 Windmill Road, in spite of the building's proximity to the railway track and the harbour, rather than the road. A few of the employees and some crewmembers of CS *Edouard Jeramec* married local girls, while others brought their families from France or Saint-Pierre and Miquelon to live in Dartmouth in the neighbourhood of their employment. Senior citizens of today still remember these French families and their children who were classmates in Victoria and Park schools in Dartmouth.

French Cable Wharf, circa 1956

In spite of the explosion, the French Cable Wharf served well for years as a docking place for other ships. It seems to have been taken over by the federal government, either during or before the Second World War.

As for the French Cable Building itself, it was taken over by the Defence Research Establishment in 1975 and completely renovated. By this time, the building was deteriorating after almost sixty years of use. The Department of National Defence decided to demolish it and have the area environmentally decontaminated. During its lifetime the wharf had housed a coal-fired heating plant and an underground fuel line for refuelling ships. The wharf was demolished by Envirosoil Limited in recent years, and after the removal of all the contaminants, the site was filled with rock and gravel so that the area would be useful for storage or parking in future.

Oland Brewery

Foundation of the Oland Brewery

Following the railway tracks north of the Compagnie Française des Cables Télégraphiques, there is a large grassy hill topped by a modern apartment building. Hidden in the shrubbery down close to the tracks are the remains of a foundation and an old brick wall. These are all that remain of what was once a substantial brewery owned by the Oland family of Dartmouth. It was referred to sometimes as the Army and Navy Brewers, sometimes as the Halifax Brewery. It was built in 1867 on what had formerly been the tan yard of Samuel Albro, with John J. D. Oland as manager, backed by several wealthy shareholders. A house was attached to the brewery, where the manager lived with his wife, Susannah, and their four children.

The brewery flourished until it totally collapsed in the explosion. Three men were killed in the building: Conrad G. Oland, William Dumaresq, and Charles Shrum. Dumaresq was the father of the unfortunate family that was so devastated on Indian Road.

Dr. John Martin adds an interesting detail about salvage at the brewery just after the explosion: "The large cedar storage vats were undamaged. Workmen pumped out 5 000

The Oland Brewery post-explosion

gallons of brew from the 12 vats and transported it to the Duke Street plant in Halifax." That would have been a disappointment for anyone hoping to siphon off some ale for private consumption, but probably few people were thinking about any such thing in the aftermath of the catastrophe.

Windmill Road

Windmill Road had a variety of homes before the explosion, some small and modest, others large and elegant, most situated on the upper side of the road to take advantage of the harbour view. Few escaped damage, either from the blast itself or by fires from overturned stoves. Numerous accounts tell of children being sent home from schools, teachers at the time having no idea of the devastation they would encounter on their walk. They would pass severely injured people and dead bodies, houses collapsed in a heap of rubble or burning fiercely. The shocking sights would cause even the stoutest hearts to grow more and more fearful as they approached their own homes.

A badly damaged Windmill Road home

One boy who arrived to see his home in terrible condition was Ian Forsyth, who had walked from the Halifax County Academy and crossed on the ferry. He entered

Ian Forsyth's home

the house with dread, and found it empty. What thoughts he must have had! Fortunately, at his aunt's house nearby he found his mother, injured but alive. Later, the whole family was reunited. Similar scenes were repeated all over town, and were never forgotten by the scarred children.

A classic etching of the Red Mill

Hester Street ran parallel to Windmill Road a block further from the harbour. It, too, had some large, attractive homes that were damaged beyond repair. Three of them were owned by branches of the Mitchell family. One of these was repaired, and remains as a reminder of the earlier architecture of the era among the newer houses built to replace those destroyed in the explosion.

Crathorne's mill

A little further south on Windmill Road, near where the comparatively modern St. Paul's Roman Catholic Church stands today, there was once a large windmill, known as the Red Mill, built late in the 1700s. This was the structure that gave the road its name. The mill was demolished in 1896, but at the foot of nearby Jamieson Street, at the harbour's edge, Crathorne's gristmill was later located, and still another mill existed on the south side of Jamieson Street, opposite the beginning of Hester Street. All these mills used water power from the stream that ran down to the harbour from Albro Lake. Crathorne's mill had a big waterwheel activating the two horizontal millstones that ground the grain.

Both the Crathorne house and mill were severely damaged by the explosion. The mill never operated again, but in the days that followed, when housing was at a premium, the Crathorne home was repaired. New tenants lived in it for a few years until it was destroyed by a fire. Large apartment houses are now found in the area.

The Naval Armament Depot, near where Imo *was beached in 1917*

The beached Imo

Naval Armament Depot

For years, naval ships collected their water supplies in casks at the foot of Jamieson Street, where water from Albro's brook flowed down to the harbour, carried by a wooden aqueduct. By the time of the explosion, however, piped water was supplied to ships from wharves in downtown Dartmouth.

Imo was beached near the present wharf of the Naval Armament Depot, either blown across the harbour by the force of the explosion or washed across on the tsunami. Although the ship was not severely damaged, its crew was not as fortunate as the men of *Mont Blanc.* Captain From, Pilot Hayes, and five crewmembers were killed. After being taken off their ship, some survivors were moved to hospital, and three of them were able to attend the inquiry into the collision just six days after the disaster.

As for *Imo,* it languished on the Dartmouth shore with a security guard until the following summer, when it was refloated and repaired. But December proved to be an unlucky month for the ship. Four years later, early in December, it foundered and sank near the Falkland Islands.

continued on page 100

Damage to North End houses

A newly married young Dartmouth couple, Arthur and Gertrude (Wright) Pettipas, lived in their attractive new home at the corner of Dawson Street and Windmill Road, straight across the harbour from the burning *Mont Blanc*. Mrs. Pettipas had a remarkable escape from death during the explosion. She was alone in the house at the time and raised her bedroom window to talk to women on the street corner below when she heard the first small explosions. She later had a detailed account of her experiences published in the *Windsor Tribune*.

According to Mrs. Pettipas, fire shot up from the burning ship, and the enormous shockwave from the blast threw her across the room. But in spite of the extensive damage to the house, the shattered glass and falling plaster, she gathered herself together, propped the burning hall stove up with a brick under a missing leg, and went out into the street. Water was dripping from the roofs of the houses from the tidal wave, which she had not even noticed in her stunned state. She saw that the new Emmanuel Church across Dawson Street was completely wrecked. She worried about her mother, who lived further north on Hester Street, so she walked hurriedly in that direction, through "black hail, great lumps of ice, coated in black soot," as well as "lumps of twisted metal." She passed horrible sights of dazed and bleeding victims looking out of their wrecked houses. A woman passed her a baby to rush to a doctor, but Gertrude persuaded the drivers of a team to take the baby to a doctor downtown.

Finally reaching her mother's house, she found it on fire, but learned to her relief that her mother had left for Halifax earlier in the morning. Making her way back to her own home, she was soon reunited with both her mother and her husband. Arthur Pettipas had suffered minor injuries, but he joined the Dartmouth Relief Committee that was formed that very morning. The couple had no children, but became prominent in town affairs during their lifetimes, with Arthur serving on town council and as mayor of Dartmouth from 1948 to 1950. Gertrude was buried in the Tufts Cove Cemetery, where many explosion victims were previously laid to rest.

Tufts Cove Cemetery

The Pettipas house today (Emmanuel Church in background)

continued from page 98

Imo was not the only ship to go aground on the Dartmouth side of the harbour. Rear Admiral Chambers of the Royal Navy toured the harbour in a tugboat immediately after the explosion to take stock of the damage. He reported in *The Naval Review* of August 1920:

> About the centre of Tufts Cove was the wreck of the fine steamer *Curaca* which had been lying at the wharf on the Richmond side (Pier 8) loading mules. She had been carried across either by the explosion or the resulting wave. Her mast and funnel were broken short off, and her stern was bulged inwards like a dented tin can. This ship must have been very close to the *Mont Blanc* at the time of the explosion.

Curaca had sunk at Tufts Cove. Forty-five crewmembers were killed, but the ship was refloated in 1918.

Old Mill Tavern

Two or three blocks above and parallel to Windmill Road was the site of a very important industry, the Dartmouth Ropewalk Company. Its existence was partly responsible for a period of rapid growth in the history of the north end of Dartmouth. Today, with car dealerships and fast food outlets dominating Wyse Road, those driving or walking along its northern end probably take very little notice of the rather shabby rectangular brick building that houses the Old Mill Tavern. It is difficult today to realize that this building was once the centrepiece of one of the largest industrial complexes in the Maritimes.

Old Mill Tavern

The ropewalk was founded by the firm of William Stairs, Son and Morrow, which already had it own fleet of sailing ships and a thriving chandlery business on the Halifax side of the harbour. In 1867 the firm purchased a large amount of land in North End Dartmouth and drew up the plans for the ropeworks, which opened for business in 1869.

At first it was simply the Dartmouth Ropewalk Company, a branch of Stairs, Son and Morrow, with partners William J. Stairs; his sons, John F. and George; and his brother–in–law, Robert Morrow. The business occupied about ten acres of land between Wyse Road and Victoria Road. What is now the Old Mill Tavern was the main building and behind it was the longest building in Nova Scotia—the ropewalk itself. Here, about four hundred yards of any kind of rope could be twisted by machine. The site also had a tarring building, an oakum factory, storage buildings, and the manager's house. Nearby, on Pelzant Street, were homes for some of the workers. John F. Stairs occupied the manager's house, which was called Northbrook.

Dartmouth Ropewalk Company

The Stairs family's holding company was called the Dartmouth Manufacturing Company Limited. It oversaw the development of new streets, where housing for its employees could be rented or bought with reasonable mortgages. Two of the new streets, John and George, were named for the sons of the family. Nine identical houses on George Street faced Victoria Park on land donated by the Stairs family and several homeowners for purposes of recreation. This park is still a pleasant open space today.

Dartmouth Ropewalk Company

The identical houses known as the "Seven Sisters"

There were three hundred employees at the ropeworks in the early 1900s, which, under the guidance of John F. Stairs, had merged with other cordage companies in the Maritimes and Quebec to form Consumers' Cordage. A superintendent with expertise in Scotland, John Moir, was brought to Dartmouth with his family in 1889. His brother, James Moir, followed circa 1889 or 1890, and since that time the Moir name has been prominent, not only in the north end, but throughout Dartmouth and further afield. When John Stairs was elected to the federal parliament, managers were brought in who lived in Northbrook with their families. First came another Scot, John Drury, who died in 1914. Next was Dartmouth-born Leo Graham, who was in the managerial position during the explosion.

While it might seem strange that property for the business had not been developed nearer the harbour and the railway that ran along it, there was a very good reason for this. The ropeworks machinery was run by water power and a dam was built on Albro Lake for this purpose. The Stairs' wharf was located at the foot of Jamieson Street near the Crathorne mill. From there, all the raw materials needed for the manufacture of rope were hauled uphill to Wyse Road, and the final product was delivered by teams returning to the wharf.

Main ropeworks building

Main ropeworks building

In spite of being further inland than the brewery, the ropeworks and many of its employees' homes suffered great damage in the explosion. The main building lost its roof and windows. Manager Leo Graham and employee George Ferguson each lost an eye, and there were many injuries amongst the employees because of shattered glass and falling bricks and timbers. The manager's house was destroyed and so were several of the smaller buildings and sheds. Northbrook was later rebuilt and still exists today. As for the large main building, its entire fourth floor was removed and a new roof covered the third floor.

Workers' homes suffered greatly. Several houses on Pelzant Street were badly damaged, caught fire, and burned to the ground. Throughout the area, people who were not injured went to work immediately to sweep up plaster and glass, and to

Isabel (Grey) Horne, now 101 years old, remembers the day of the explosion as if it were yesterday. Her home with her aunt and uncle, Mr. and Mrs. John Cox, was on the corner of Windmill Road and Pelzant Street. They had come from Dundee in 1912 to work at Consumers' Cordage, bringing their niece, Isabel, who was seven, with them. By 1917 she was in a classroom of Central School in downtown Dartmouth, when the explosion severely damaged the school. Isabel's only thought was to get home. With other friends, she took her usual shortcut across Dartmouth Park, past Park School, along what is now Wyse Road, and down Pelzant Street to the corner. The roof of Isabel's home was gone, but the kitchen was in fair shape. Her aunt and uncle were there, and so were several neighbours who had been wounded. Mrs. Cox was doing her best to attend to them because she had a reputation in the neighbourhood for being able to help in medical emergencies.

When word came of the possibility of another explosion, Isabel went with other children to sit around a bonfire in Dartmouth Park until it began to get dark. By five o'clock they were all hungry, so Isobel ventured into a neighbourhood store that had been damaged, and found two boxes of biscuits, which she shared with the others.

Going home then, she found her uncle had put a mattress on the kitchen floor and surrounded it with tarpaper. They tried to sleep there, but it began to snow, and all the children in the neighbourhood were gathered up and taken to bunk houses at Imperoyal.

The Coxes moved to Halifax, living with relatives until their Dartmouth home was rebuilt. By that time, Isabel was going to Halifax County Academy, going over on the ferry each day.

cover the windows with whatever material they could find. But they were the lucky ones. It was estimated that 162 houses in Dartmouth, most of them in the North End, were unliveable, entirely ruined.

The damaged Emmanuel Church of England

Emmanuel Church of England

Soon after their ropeworks had started production, the Stairs family had a small building put up in the grounds for meeting purposes, schooling, and church services. Later a larger building was erected on the corner of Dawson and George streets, known as Stairs Church. It was used on Sundays for Presbyterian services, and on Thursday nights for Church of England adherents.

In 1913, however, the new Emmanuel Church of England, designed by architect William Critchlow Harris, was opened at the corner of Windmill Road and Dawson Street, and so for a short time Anglicans and Presbyterians had their own churches. But, as Gertrude Pettipas wrote in her account of the explosion, Emmanuel was "a heap of ruins" after the blast. By 1920, a second Emmanuel church, designed by architect R. A. Johnson, who had previously designed the French Cable Building, was completed on the same site that the former church had occupied.

The second Emmanuel Church of England

Stairs Memorial Church

By the time the Emmanuel adherents moved to their new church, Presbyterians were finding the old Dawson Street Church not only too small, but also draughty after it had been repaired. The congregation worked hard to raise money for a new church, which was eventually built on a lot of land at the corner of Henry and Hester streets, and constructed of concrete. In 1922 the building was opened and named Stairs Memorial Church to honour the family that had done so much to promote the growth of north end Dartmouth. Gertrude Pettipas contributed the bell for the church. Today another church congregation occupies this building, while the newest Stairs Memorial Church on nearby Hester Street overlooks it.

Damaged Stairs Church

The new Stairs Memorial Church

Bethel Baptist Church

Across Windmill Road from Turtle Grove, where the tall towers of the power corporation are today, stood the Bethel Baptist Mission Church, supported by the First Baptist Church of downtown Dartmouth. It was completely destroyed by the explosion, but its minister and the congregation cleared up the debris and managed to rebuild it and have the new church open for services by 1921.

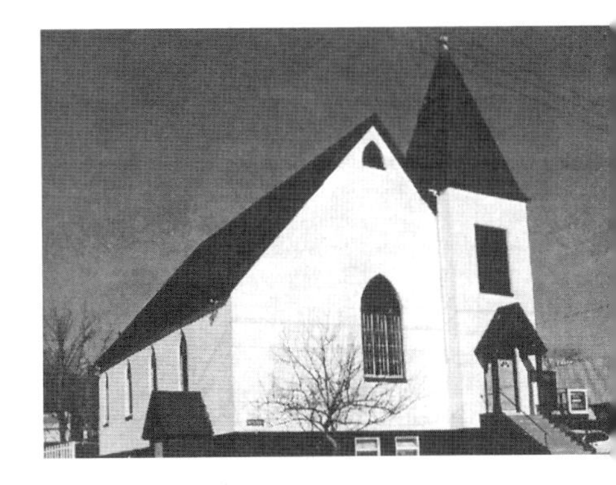

The rebuilt Bethel Baptist Church

The large pieces of steel from the exploding *Mont Blanc* that flew in all directions included its heavy, twisted, red-hot cannon, which landed more than three miles away from *Mont Blanc* near Little Albro Lake. The land there was owned by the Stairs' Dartmouth Manufacturing Company. At the Dartmouth town council meeting in February 1918, the company offered the cannon as a gift to the town, provided it be put on a site within the town. As a result, it spent

Mont Blanc's cannon

some time on the grounds of Greenvale School, then moved to the post office, after which it was relegated to the town workshop. Former Dartmouth mayor A. C. Johnston, fearing that the cannon might end up as scrap, had it removed to his own residence at the top of Wentworth Street for safekeeping. After his death and the subsequent sale of his property, the cannon was moved to Westphal and eventually became the property of Colonel Sidney Oland of Halifax. He donated it to the Dartmouth Heritage Museum, which was located on Wyse Road. There it was mounted in front of the building, with a suitable plaque telling its story.

Mont Blanc Memorial Park

Mont Blanc Memorial Park

Today, through the efforts of dedicated Dartmouthians, the mounted barrel of *Mont Blanc's* cannon forms the centrepiece of the Mont Blanc Memorial Park at the corner of Albro Lake Road and Pinecrest Drive in north end Dartmouth, very near the spot where it landed on the day of the explosion. On the cannon's left is a plaque with the names of people who were killed in Dartmouth by the explosion. One name, Yves Gueguiner, has a poignant connection with the site; he was the gunner of *Mont Blanc,* in charge of the cannon now adjacent to the plaque that bears his name. (He was the French sailor who made it to shore safely but suffered shrapnel injuries and died from loss of blood.) Ninety-four names are listed on the plaque, the majority of them belonging to people who were killed in north Dartmouth and Tufts Cove.

The plaque with the names of those who died in Dartmouth and Tufts Cove

On the right of the cannon is a second plaque showing *Imo* and telling the story of the explosion. Because so many of the names on the plaque are those of the people of Tufts Cove and the north end of Dartmouth, the site of the Memorial Park was chosen with care.

Each year on the morning of December 6, a service is held at the park to remember that terrible day and the people whose lives were cut short or irrevocably changed. The Dartmouth service was inspired by the one held in Halifax each year. Looking straight across the harbour from Albro Lake Road one sees the jagged outline of the memorial bell tower, standing out on the skyline atop the hill at Fort Needham, site of Halifax's annual memorial service.

The Nova Scotia Hospital

For all its sense of community, the north end of Dartmouth lacked the benefit of medical facilities in 1917. The injured who could walk found their way to downtown Dartmouth in search of doctors. There were few cars in 1917, but horse-drawn delivery wagons, children's carts, baby carriages, and even wheelbarrows were put to use to transport people

continued on page 109

The Nova Scotia Hospital

Dalhousie Professor Archibald MacMechan had been asked to be the director of the Halifax Disaster Record Office. His collection of explosion records was never published, but among his papers is the following personal narrative (now held in Nova Scotia's Public Archives), which he collected from Dr. Matthew Burris. MacMechan's notes are a graphic record of the hectic pace one physician kept up for several days immediately following the disaster:

"At nine o'clock was just getting up. Shaving. Felt the house shake and felt that something terrible had happened. Thought that there was a bombardment of some kind. The explosion was low, not so loud as the noon-day gun, and he thought that it was a shell from a submarine. His little daughter, downstairs, screamed. A second explosion was louder but still, there was no breaking of glass. He was sure now that it was a bombardment. Ran downstairs, caught up his little girl and called to his wife and the maid to come to the cellar...They were all in the cellar when the 'big' explosion came. Everything smashed. After waiting some time for more, Dr. B. came upstairs. Went into office, a man was there with his face cut—wanted Dr. B. to dress it. Soon many people were there to be 'fixed up'. Only small hurts came first, as Dr. B. lives near the ferry and people were not so badly injured in that part of Dartmouth. Later, people from the North End came and were much worse hurt. One child had his skull fractured, broken like an eggshell—the brain substance was oozing down over the side of his face—he lived about three weeks. A man in uniform warned them of a second explosion, 'Worse, far worse than the first.' There were fifteen or twenty people in the office then. They all went away. Dr. B. took his wife and child in his car to an open space about five or six hundred yards up the street. Went back to the house. Took all the food he could find and put it in a big bread-box, put milk in a stone jug. Took them to the back yard and buried them under stones from the stone wall. Got his account books and wrapped them in the automobile cover and buried them under stones...

Then he put on fires and got plenty of hot water ready. He was in the office dressing injuries for the rest of the day, as people began coming in again very soon. His wife and child came back about one o'clock. Worked all afternoon, and after he had had some tea, began to visit homes and do what he could for people. Kept this up until 2 AM and then went down to N.S. Hospital where he knew Dr. Lawlor was alone. There were 250 patients there, in the building which had been used as an infectious hospital. When all the cases had been attended to, Dr. B. went back home and worked for a couple of hours fixing up his house so that it would be comparatively storm-proof..."

Dr. Matthew Burris's Dartmouth home

continued from page 107

who needed medical care. The five doctors who lived around King and Queen streets were almost instantly overwhelmed by the necessity of tending to wounded, burned, and dying patients. Like the crews on the ferry boats, Doctors Burris, Dickson, Gandier, Payzant, and Smith were genuine heroes of the day.

Two hundred and fifty injured and homeless people had been taken to the Nova Scotia Hospital. The main dining room, the upstairs recreation room, and any other available spaces were being utilized as well. Finally, in the evening, nine doctors arrived, including Dr. Matthew Burris. Others in the group were Dartmouthian Dr. William Hattie (a former superintendent of the Nova Scotia Hospital, but at the time Inspector of Humane Institutions), two Army Medical Corps doctors, another Dartmouth physician, and four Nova Scotians from other communities who had arrived to help in the emergency.

Dr. George Gandier, an eye, ear, nose, and throat specialist whose office was a little further east on Queen Street, was also extremely busy. At least fifteen people in Dartmouth and Tufts Cove lost one eye or the sight of an eye. Dr. Gandier attended to their needs to the best of his ability in the fearful crisis situation, during which one person had lost both eyes.

Two people who were not successful in getting medical attention in time died when their throats were cut by glass.

Greenvale School

Not only doctors were busy. Concerned citizens gathered at the Dartmouth Ferry Terminal on the morning of the explosion and formed the Dartmouth Relief Committee. The committee moved to several locations during its existence, relocating next to the

continued on page 111

Greenvale School

Fairview, pictured today

Edith (Barss) Baker lived with her husband, Harold, on the crest of the hill on Victoria Road in her late father's house, called Fairview. After looking around at the damage done to the house, she worried about her eighty-four-year-old grandmother, Mary Jane Payzant, who lived with her son, Dr. Allison Payzant, on Queen Street. Edith and Harold walked downtown, observing conditions of the houses they passed on the way. Not until they entered Dr. Payzant's house did they fully realize the seriousness of whatever it was that had happened. The doctor's house was filled with patients, nurses, and doctors hurrying back and forth. Grandmother Payzant had been taken next door. Edith and Harold gathered her up and walked her, protesting, the long way up the steep hill to their own house. Edith Baker related these events in a letter to two of her brothers, Walter and Geoffrey, who were serving overseas, and the letter is now preserved in the Dartmouth Heritage Museum.

Mollie (Wilson) Forbes described Dr. Dickson's day to interviewer Lois Richards: "Dr. Dickson was a hero. The windows in his home were blown out and he moved his big dining room table outside to the square where he worked all day and into the night sewing up people and cleaning their wounds."

Harriet Bishop, a Dartmouth nurse, helped Dr. Dickson on King Street that day. In a letter to her relatives, Robert and Lorna Huestis, she wrote: "It was a nightmare—operating on sidewalks with Dr. Dickson and on the day after the explosion wading around in snow and having to leave in the midst of it to attend to my brother, B. O. Bishop, with broken ribs. It's a wonder I didn't have ulcers of the stomach or something. Guess I was too busy night and day to think. Had to deliver babies, one a breach presentation and baptize it too, in case it didn't survive."

continued from page 109

former brick post office at the corner of Water Street (now Alderney Drive) and Ferry Hill, then to Greenvale School, and lastly to Christ Church parish hall. The chairman of the committee was A. C. Johnston, former mayor of Dartmouth. Subcommittees were formed: shelter, food, fuel, transportation, clothing, building, patrol, animals, information, care of bodies, salvage, and executive. A. F. Baker was appointed secretary. His wife and Mrs. F. J. Ward were the only women named on the committee, but probably many others were helping behind the scenes. Edith Baker and her husband, Harold, were both working for the relief committee.

The names of male committee members read like a who's who of Dartmouth society at the time, as they were the same people who organized Natal Day activities and the fairs held in aid of British relief. The formation of the relief committee was an amazingly quick response to the emergency situation. Needless to say, it had great demands placed upon it, the most urgent being for food, shelter, and clothing for the homeless, medical care for the injured, and funeral arrangements for the dead.

In addition to Greenvale School and the Nova Scotia Hospital, Edgemere, a house on Crichton Avenue, was turned over by its owners as a temporary hospital. Today, it is part of a seniors' housing development, but in 1917 it was owned by Emily and Henry Rosenberg. Emily Rosenberg had inherited the magnificent house from her father. Henry Rosenberg was the retired principal of the Victoria School of Art and Design.

Two years before the explosion, Edgemere had been in the news in a Dartmouth newspaper, but most Dartmouthians have never heard this story. It was a rather startling one to a grade four teacher several years ago when she took her class on a walking tour of Dartmouth on a warm day in June, near the end of the school year. As they passed Edgemere, a little girl pointed up to its round tower, which overlooks the town and harbour. "A German spy lived up there during the war," she announced. "He had a telescope and watched the ships in the harbour."

Her teacher had not heard this story before, but Dartmouth historian Harry Chapman traced the rumour back to a 1915 Dartmouth newspaper. Nothing further came of it, but the story obviously pointed to Henry Rosenberg, whose name sounded German, and who perhaps owned a telescope. What would be more natural and fascinating for a man of leisure than to watch the comings and goings of ships in the harbour, especially in wartime?

Edgemere today

Beechwood

Beechwood

Beechwood, the large home of the late Dr. Parker on Pleasant Street near the Old Ferry Road, also gave refuge to explosion victims. Later, it was used as a contagious diseases hospital and then as a tuberculosis hospital. When it outlived its usefulness for this purpose, it was demolished.

The Imperial Oil Refinery also provided refuge. It had empty bunkhouses, which had recently been occupied by construction workers while the refinery was erected. The bunkhouses were able to house 68 homeless women and 116 children until January 12. The refinery provided trained nurses and a caretaker, and also donated generously to the relief fund.

The light tower

While the north end and Tufts Cove had certainly been hit the hardest, especially in regard to deaths and injuries, there was a great deal of property damage in downtown Dartmouth and lesser amounts in the suburbs of Woodside, Woodlawn, Westphal, and Cole Harbour. In the town itself, there was hardly a window left whole. Chimneys were cracked or collapsed and some homes were left with gaping corners where walls had been forced apart. Churches and schools suffered considerable damage.

As the extent of the damage was realized, there were some ironic twists of fate. Since 1884, Dartmouthians had skated on a splendid indoor rink at the top of Synott's Hill, at the corner of Wyse and Windmill roads. As the home of the Chebucto Amateur Athletic Hockey Team, it was the scene of highly competitive hockey games. For general skating sessions, a local orchestra, the Harpers, played excellent music for skaters. Combined with reduced ferry fares, the smooth ice surface, and the music of the Harpers, the rink lured even members of the Halifax Skating Club to Dartmouth for its weekly sessions. A high tower topped the entranceway, enclosing a range light to guide ships coming into Halifax Harbour. However, less than a week before the explosion a newspaper held a significant item from the minutes of the town council: "A steel frame lighthouse is being built on a cliff on the west side of Windmill Road. It may be finished before the end of the year. The lighthouse at the Dartmouth rink has been condemned, and was only temporary anyway. It has been weakened by storms."

The skating rink at Wyse and Windmill roads

Councillors must have been astonished when they surveyed the rink after the explosion. It was completely flattened, except for the supposedly weakened light tower, which still stood defiantly straight and tall in spite of its battering.

Since the explosion, however, a new range light on a steel frame has stood on the harbour side of Windmill Road at the top of Synott's Hill. It is situated above the cemetery of St. Paul's Roman Catholic Church.

The new range light tower in Dartmouth Park

Hawthorne School

Another similar irony concerned the town schools. At the time, overcrowding was a serious problem. The original wooden Greenvale School had been totally destroyed by fire just three years before, in 1914. Dartmouth's school board at that time contacted well-known architect Andrew Cobb, noted for his recent work on Dalhousie's then-new Studley Campus, and invited him to draw up plans, not only for a new brick Greenvale, but for a brick Hawthorne School as well.

The two new schools, Greenvale and Hawthorne, had recently opened in 1915, but the town health officer, Dr. Payzant, was still not happy. In the town's annual report

Hawthorne School

published in early 1917, he had written firmly, "Central and Park Schools are a blot on civilization and should be removed as soon as possible." Neither of these schools had electricity or running water. Children used outhouses at the back of their playgrounds, which were divided by fences into separate areas for girls and boys. A plebiscite had been held to sanction the borrowing of money for a new brick school in the Dartmouth Park, but the voters turned it down with a casual lack of concern for the unsavoury hygienic conditions that their children endured. However, Dr. Payzant got his wish in the end, because both Central and Park schools, although not totally demolished, were unfit for use as schools, shaken as they were to their very foundations.

Park School

The old, wooden Park School stood on an exposed hill on Wyse Road across from the flattened rink. After the explosion, the school was used as a temporary morgue for a very short time. It was deemed unsafe for classes, so there was no choice but to construct the new brick school that had such a short time ago been voted down in the plebiscite. The new school was designed by architect A. Graham Creighton and built by Antigonish contractor W. E. Landry. It was closed in 1982 and demolished a few years later.

The old wooden school was rented to the local militia on the condition that they made the necessary repairs. Between the two world wars, it served as an armouries for the eighty-seventh and eighty-eighth artillery batteries, and next as the site where the Dartmouth Gliding Club put together its first glider in 1946.

Dartmouth's population mushroomed after the opening of the Angus L. Macdonald Bridge in 1955. The Mechanics' Institute on Ochterloney Street had served as a town hall for years, but was by this time inadequate for the burgeoning population. So that historic old building fell to the wrecker's hammer and a new town hall opened on the site of the former wooden Park School in December 1957.

Just four years later, Dartmouth amalgamated with its suburbs and became a city. Suddenly the new town hall seemed woefully inadequate, and a splendid new city hall on Ferry Hill replaced it. However, a great benefit to Dartmouth occurred in Canada's Centennial Year, 1967, when the Dartmouth Regional Library and the new Dartmouth Heritage Museum moved into the building on Synott's Hill with its magnificent panoramic view. Both of these institutions have now moved out, and the once much-admired town hall is boarded up with an uncertain future due to construction and health problems.

Old Park School and the Dartmouth rink and light tower

A. Graham Creighton's new Park School

These two choice sites that had held the much-loved rink and two Park Schools, today play no role in Dartmouth life.

Central School

Central School opened on Queen Street on the site of the original Quaker Meeting house shortly after the passing of the Free School Act in 1864. It served the town well, but for its pupils and teachers the explosion was a blessing because this "blot on civilization" was closed forever as a school. Grace Church was permitted to use it for temporary storage after the explosion, and then the Bluebell Athletic Association and later the Dartmouth Boys' Christian Association held their meetings in the old building, but it was finally razed in 1922. Today it is the site of a parking lot for the main Dartmouth Post Office.

Central School

Victoria School

Two-roomed Victoria School on Wyse Road lost windows and was considerably shaken by the explosion. However, architect A. Graham Creighton designed a second storey, added a new roof, and improved the heating system, which enabled Victoria School to serve the elementary pupils of north Dartmouth for many additional years. The land it once stood on is now part of a strip mall.

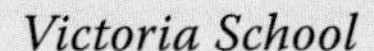

Victoria School

Graham Creighton's improved Victoria School

Christ Church Parish Hall

There was much difficulty in finding spots for all the students displaced by the explosion. Even the two new brick schools needed windows replaced, and Greenvale was occupied by the Dartmouth Relief Committee. It is interesting to note that while the emergency situation lasted, each subcommittee had its own phone line at Greenvale. This technology must have been revolutionary in 1917—six telephones in one building! There were great demands for help placed on the workers and the lines were extremely busy. By mid-January 1918 the crisis was somewhat less urgent, and the whole committee moved to Christ Church Parish Hall. Near the end of the month, with complicated scheduling difficulties, including morning and afternoon shifts, all the children in the town were accommodated in the two brick schools—Greenvale and Hawthorne.

Christ Church Parish Hall, home of the Dartmouth Relief Committee

The site today

Sterns Corner, Portland Street, boarded up after the explosion

Sterns Corner today

Sterns Corner, Portland Street, boarded up after the explosion

Sterns Corner

Businesses along Dartmouth's shoreline were badly damaged, including foundries, the paint factory, ferry terminals, boat builders, the molasses factory, and the skate factory and its rolling mill near the entrance to the canal. In Dartmouth cove, USS *Morrill,* a coast guard patrol vessel, moored as it waited to take on supplies, sustained much damage to its superstructure. Grocery stores were plentiful on Portland, Water, and Ochterloney streets. Spears of glass pierced goods inside, even canned goods, making it necessary to dispose of much of the grocers' stock.

St. Peter's Church on Maple Street

St. Peter's Church

Like the north end churches, downtown churches were in a shambles. Old St. Peter's Roman Catholic Church on Chapel Lane (now Edward Street), which had originally been rowed over from Halifax after St. Mary's Basilica replaced it, had many broken windows. So did the new brick St.

Peter's Church on Maple Street. The high wooden St. Peter's Hall on Ochterloney Street, next to the old church, had structural damage because of its height. All of these buildings have since disappeared and been replaced by the round St. Peter's Church designed by architect Graham Hooper. It is located on Crichton Avenue near the corner of Ochterloney Street. St. Peter's Hall has been replaced by a Tim Horton's. The St. Peter's Church pictured was burned in a spectacular fire in 1966.

The new Grace Methodist Church

Grace Methodist Church

Grace Methodist Church with its two spires on the southeast corner of King and Ochterloney Streets was severely affected. The congregation attempted to hold services in the basement, but found it necessary to rebuild the church entirely. While construction was underway, Central School was used to store salvageable contents of the original church, and the school's playground held building materials for the new church. L. R. Fairn was the architect. Strong, attractive yellow brick was chosen as the building material. During the construction period, the Grace congregation met in the assembly hall of Greenvale School for prayer meeting one evening a week, and for the Sunday church service as well. The new church opened in June 1920.

Old Baptist Church

One block further south on King Street, the Baptist church was also mortally wounded. A gaping hole in its roof left hope for a brief while that the church might be salvaged, but very soon the entire roof collapsed. Church services were held in the church hall next door, as the congregation considered future plans. Andrew Cobb, who had been the architect for Greenvale and Hawthorne schools, designed a fine new church us-

New Baptist Church

ing attractive fieldstone for its exterior. It was built on a lot of land at the southwest corner of Ochterloney Street and Victoria Road. This location had the added advantage of an existing house on one end of the lot, which could serve as the parsonage. The new church was dedicated in September 1922.

Christ Church Anglican

The oldest Dartmouth church is the Anglican Christ Church, whose cornerstone was laid in 1817. One hundred years later, in the summer of 1917, its centennial was celebrated by its parishioners. By then the church was well established, well cared for, and had several beautiful stained glass windows. Then, at the end of that same year, came the explosion. The entire structure was badly

Old Baptist Church

Old Baptist Church damaged after the explosion

shaken, its frame twisted, the stained glass windows broken, and the chimneys cracked. Fortunately, the recently built church hall was not as badly damaged, so it was repaired first and used for Sunday services until 1919, when the congregation moved back into the restored church.

Christ Church Anglican

Presbyterian Church of St. James

The Presbyterian Church of St. James, built in 1871, stood on a high knoll at the corner of Prince Albert Road and Portland Street, probably the most exposed location of all central Dartmouth churches. Already, in 1892, its tall steeple had been removed, due to its vulnerability to the winds of strong southerly storms from the sea. In retrospect this was a fortunate decision. Surprisingly, though, the damage to the church and manse was not as bad as might have been expected in that location.

Christ Church today

Minutes of meetings held in the basement hall of St. James on December 16 are tantalizingly vague, but what they do reveal is that an agreement was made to use the basement as living quarters for reconstruction workers who had flocked to Dartmouth to help with restoration efforts. There is no record of how many workers lived in the basement, but conditions must have been primitive, for there were only two toilets, two sinks, and no bathtubs or showers. The workers stayed until the end of April.

Because the hall was taken up by workmen, arrangements were made for church organizations to unite with other churches for weekly prayer meetings; the Mission Band used basement rooms in the rear of the church; the Boy Scouts looked for space in Greenvale School or Christ Church Parish Hall; and the Young People's Society met in people's homes.

But when the workers left, a bill "was presented from the janitor for cleaning and fumigating the basement...The Secretary was instructed to write to the Relief Commission asking why the basement had not been cleaned and why five tons of coal had not been replaced, all as agreed. A bill for the coal and the janitor's expenses was to be attached."

Presbyterian Church of St. James

The church held its first services on December 23, and other congregations were invited to attend. Glass for the windows, costing around five hundred dollars, was ordered on February 11, but was not installed until the summer.

The Starr Factory's rolling mill

The Starr Factory, which lay in a direct line between St. James and the harbour, was completely destroyed and never rebuilt. This is an odd twist of fate, given that the factory was low and sturdily constructed, while St. James stood high up on its knoll, exposed to the harbour.

The Dartmouth Relief Committee, set up by volunteers on the very morning of the explosion, worked day and night to ease the terrible plight of people who had lost the necessities of life. Of forty families in Tufts Cove, thirty-eight were in dire straits. The relief committee found shelter for as many as possible and set up three food stations within the town. On the Sunday following the explosion, December 9, A. C. Pettipas, who was in charge of the No. 2 station, reported that twenty-two families were served in two hours. But there were rumours that the rules for obtaining food were too strict, which was unnecessarily cruel at a time when there were people almost dying from lack of nourishment.

The Starr Factory's rolling mill

One cannot help but wonder if the committee members living in the comfort of Greenvale School, with meals provided, had any idea of the true state of those unfortunate souls who had literally lost everything. Though the volunteers had the best of intentions, they had no real experience of disasters and how to deal with them. This, for instance, is the statement of the Food Committee in the *Relief Committee Bulletin*:

> The Food Committee have had numerous demands made upon them for relief from persons that, in the judgment of the Committee, are well able to provide for themselves. In any instance where the head of the family is in good health and capable of earning a livelihood the Food Commission absolutely refuse to supply provisions. In any case where relief is needed the head of the family must apply to the Food Committee unless unable to do so, in which case an order from the head of the family must accompany the request. In future where the Committee are in doubt as to the necessity of relief a representative of the Committee will make a personal investigation. The Relief Committee

> are issuing a week's supply of food to each applicant and they will not re-issue a further supply until the expiration of that time. The Food Committee are keeping a record of all provisions issued to the different applicants.

Fortunately, the very next day American Red Cross workers arrived, including nurse Jessie Forbes of New York. She was sent to Dartmouth, bringing a practical, experienced approach to the situation. She immediately organized an extensive, two-day house-to-house registration under the chairmanship of one of the relief committee volunteers, H. Baker. Eight additional volunteers went door to door, filling in registration forms with regard to lack of food, clothing, shelter, and medical attention.

The results of this survey showed such an enormity of problems that Miss Kempshall of the New York Charity Organization Society and two nurses from Toronto's Department of Health were immediately hired. As well, two young Dartmouth women were added to the paid staff—Ethel Stanford and Adelaide Hiltz. With needs set down clearly in black and white on the registration forms, this systematic body of workers, paid by the Halifax Relief Commission, speedily provided the specific assistance needed, lessening the burden on the Dartmouth Relief Committee and allowing many of that committee's members to retire.

By December 28 the three food stations were closed, and food, fuel, and other supply orders were sent directly to dealers. The clothing department did not close until mid-February.

From early days the relationship between Dartmouth and Halifax had been rather like that of a teenaged son and his father. Dartmouth wanted its independence and resented being overruled. This fractiousness showed up in the tense days immediately following the explosion. Apparently, the Halifax Relief Committee wanted to dispose of the Dartmouth Relief Committee entirely. After a heated discussion, H. R. Silver of Dartmouth became a liaison between the two committees, requisitioning supplies through J. C. Stredder of the Halifax Supply Company.

Next came a squabble about Halifax nurses working in Dartmouth, although actually the nurses had come not directly from Halifax but from New York and Toronto.

Colonel Robert S. Low of the Halifax committee was made general manager of the reconstruction initiative. He immediately gathered together carpenters, masons, plumbers, and electricians to work on homes that were repairable and to start building temporary housing.

The town engineer of New Glasgow, E. S. Fraser, was engaged for a period of sixty days to superintend the work of the reconstruction committee in Dartmouth. (The town did not have an engineer on its staff.) In Victoria Park, six temporary wooden apartment buildings of eight units each were erected for homeless families, until single-family units could be built. They were thrown up quickly, following the design of the Halifax Reconstruction Committee. The firm of Whebby and Smith built the units in Victoria Park, and the plumbers were Ritchie and Company. The buildings were constructed of wood and tarpaper and were intended to last for only five years. Fortunately, they were equipped with electricity and running water.

Financial assistance poured into Halifax from other parts of Canada, Britain, and the United States. The sum rose to twenty-one million dollars, and it became obvious that serious planning was needed for the prudent distribution of the money. For this reason the permanent Halifax Relief Commission was formed in January 1918. There were more

Temporary apartment houses, pictured here in Halifax, were similar to the ones built in Victoria Park, Dartmouth.

Steam trains at the hydrostone plant

The hydrostone plant

petty quarrels between the volunteer committees and the permanent commission, but eventually all differences were ironed out and the permanent commission managed the financial affairs and pensions of survivors until it was disbanded in 1976.

The Hydrostone Plant

In February 1918 noted British town planner Thomas Adams came to Halifax to begin planning the Hydrostone development, as discussed in the previous chapter. Readers may be surprised to find the Hydrostone mentioned in this account of Dartmouth's explosion sites, but the eastern side of Halifax Harbour had a significant role to play in the development of the Hydrostone area, a little piece of history that is not often spoken of.

At the time of the explosion, and as late as the 1950s, a large sandy beach existed in Eastern Passage. Called Barrie Beach, and also known as Land's End, it ran parallel to the Shore Road from just north of Caldwell Road south to a fairly high headland about a quarter of a mile north of the present Second World War fort, which is now part of the Hartlen Point Forces Golf Club. The headland and the beach no longer exist due to erosion and pirating of the sand for commercial use, but they are still shown on old charts. In 1917 the fine white sand beach stretched from Shore Road for a distance of five or six hundred feet to the water's edge. A warm lagoon offered spa-like temperatures for the faint of heart, although most preferred the surf. The whole area was extremely popular on hot summer days.

Halifax homes built by the firm of Ross and Macdonald

This idyllic spot was picked for a new industry early in 1918—a plant to manufacture concrete blocks called hydrostones, as specified in Thomas Adams' plans for the redevelopment of Halifax. Today there is no vestige of the beach, the lagoon, or the factory, but there are still people who remember a derelict building, short stretches of narrow-gauge railway tracks, and two small abandoned steam trains on the northernmost part of the beach. These relics were all that remained of the once industrious hydrostone plant operated by the Nova Scotian Construction Co. Ltd.

Post-explosion homes in Dartmouth

Hydrostone blocks were made of a mixture of gravel, crushed rock, sand, and Portland cement, which was then moulded into blocks under pressure. The blocks were loaded on flat beds, hauled by one of the little steam engines to the dock close by, and transferred to barges that crossed the harbour to a similar rail line in Halifax. According to Ernest Clarke's "The Hydrostone Phoenix," included in the book *Ground Zero*, the plant could produce 3,500 to 4,000 blocks per day. Because the transportation of the concrete blocks from Eastern Passage to Halifax was an expensive proposition, the manufacturing plant was not viable once Adams's project had been completed.

The Hydrostone district was an exceptionally successful undertaking and remains today as a special attraction in Halifax. It provided 324 homes for the regeneration of North End Halifax.

However, 660 additional homes were needed in other hard-hit areas of both Halifax and Dartmouth. The Montreal firm of Ross and Macdonald, architects of the hydrostone houses, drew plans for other houses that could be altered by choosing different roof designs, porches, and building materials. Their designs were popular and accessible. Despite having additions from time to time, the houses are still recognizable in North End Halifax and Dartmouth. None of these houses are hydrostone; most were constructed of wooden beams and shingles, some were finished in stucco. Among the other architects used in Dartmouth restorations were S. P. Dumaresq, L. R. Fairn, R. A. Johnson, and Andrew Cobb. It is a fascinating project to walk or drive around the streets in North End Dartmouth—Windmill Road, Hester and Fairbanks streets, for instance—identifying the recognizable architecture of the post-explosion homes.

Conclusion

People often ask, "Did Halifax change as a result of the explosion? Were there any improvements?"

Physically, the north end of the city was very much altered. Anyone returning there in the mid twenties, after a long absence, would not have recognized it. Relief efforts brought into the city a huge influx of trained medical and social workers, town planners, builders, and engineers. New schools and hospitals improved health and education facilities. The rebuilt houses, many occupying the same sites as the destroyed ones, were supplied with conveniences that some of the old ones had lacked.

A memorial coin issued to mark the seventy-fifth anniversary of the explosion

As a result of enquiries that followed the explosion, the management of the harbour became much more efficient, making it a safer place. Industries that had taken up a large part of the harbour frontage were not replaced, like the huge sugar refinery, or were relocated, like the Richmond Printing Company. In the years immediately after the explosion, other Richmond companies rebuilt or relocated to the northern parts of Robie and Kempt Streets, but have been largely replaced with businesses connected with automobiles. The shipyards have expanded, taking more land, including some that had been occupied by North Street Station.

The two harbour bridges built in the 1950s and 70s, the Macdonald and the MacKay, have greatly changed the appearance of the harbour, connecting the two sides with busy thoroughfares. They have meant changes to approach roads and to the buildings on either end. Africville, a black community at the northern tip of Halifax, near the MacKay Bridge, is no longer there. Seaview Park now occupies most of its land. The ships seen in the modern harbour are very different from those in 1917. Cargoes have changed, and the container

The former City Club on Barrington Street, which housed various relief committees, is now used by Neptune Theatre School

ships themselves look much too large to pass through the Narrows on their way to the Fairview Container Terminal. Tall cranes now perform the task of loading and unloading the great containers with their unseen cargo; stevedores are no longer needed to perform the hard manual labour. There are fewer naval vessels in the harbour, and more pleasure boats. Large cruise ships use the piers opposite George's Island, bringing thousands of visitors to Halifax every summer. Even with the damp fog that drifts in from the Atlantic shrouding its beauty, Halifax Harbour remains one of the world's finest natural harbours.

The Fairview Container Terminal today

But the survivors of the broken families—no matter how well planned and comfortable their new housing, no matter how modern their hospitals or schools—would have exchanged all their new conveniences for the life they were living before that disastrous day of December 6, 1917.

The Dartmouth side of the harbour is vastly different than it was in 1917, largely as a result of the two cross-harbour bridges. Most of the small industries that once lined the waterfront have disappeared. Gone too are the vehicle ferries, which have been replaced by smaller passenger ferries, while the little north ferry service has disappeared altogether. The brewery and the Mi'kmaq village in Turtle Grove are no more, and although the French Cable Building is in the same location and very well preserved, it is no longer connected with the cable industry. Larger businesses and institutions are located along the shores of Dartmouth and Tufts Cove: the Canadian Coast Guard, the Naval Armament Depot, Defence Research and Development Canada Atlantic, the Nova Scotia Power thermal station, Shannon Park, and the Bedford Institute of Oceanography.

Pleasure boats in Halifax Harbour

Modern Dartmouth waterfront and passenger ferry

Halifax Harbour remains a focal point of Dartmouth, welcoming all kinds of ships and boats. Twice in recent years a magnificent armada of tall ships, sailing vessels from all over the world, have visited, treating a huge audience on both sides of the harbour to a parade of sail.

The recently launched *Queen Mary II* came into the harbour in September 2004, and as it sailed past George's Island, observers on the Dartmouth side were impressed that

Queen Mary 2

the island was completely hidden behind the liner, such was its great bulk. Another huge vessel arrived in 2006—a freighter from China, one of the new panamax ships. Too large to pass through the Suez Canal, these behemoths sail east across the Pacific and use the Panama Canal to reach the Atlantic and its ports. In Halifax Harbour the panamax ships can sail right up to the Fairview Cove container port, thanks to the harbour's famously deep waters.

Today, the vibrancy of Halifax, Dartmouth, and the harbour is a testament to those who worked so hard to rebuild after the explosion of December 1917. May these communities never again face such a terrible catastrophe.

Nova Scotia Archives and Record Management

Those seeking further explosion-related material will find a considerable amount at the Nova Scotia Archives and Record Management, on the corner of Robie Street and University Avenue.

BIBLIOGRAPHY

Books, reports, and articles

Akins, T. B. *History of Halifax City*. Halifax: Mika Publishing, 1978.

Candow, James E., ed. *Industry and Society in Nova Scotia: An Illustrated History*. Halifax: Fernwood Publishing, 2001.

Chapman, Harry. *Sketches of Old Dartmouth*. Dartmouth: Dartmouth Museum Society, 1991.

———. *Dartmouth's Day of Anguish*. Darmouth: Dartmouth Museum Society, 1992.

——— *White Shirts and Blue Collars: Industry in Dartmouth, 1785–1995*. Dartmouth: Dartmouth Historical Association, 1997.

———. *In the Wake of the Alderney: Dartmouth, Nova Scotia, 1750–2000*. Dartmouth: Dartmouth Historical Association, 2000.

Chapman, Harry, ed. *The Mustard Seeds: The Journey of Dartmouth Churches*. Dartmouth: Dartmouth Historical Association, 1999.

Drysdale, Arthur. *Drysdale Report*. Halifax: Wreck Commissioner's Court, 1918.

Erickson, Paul A. *Historic North End Halifax*. Halifax: Nimbus Publishing, 2004.

Fingard, Judith, Janet Guildford, and David Sutherland. *Halifax: The First 250 Years*. Halifax: Formac Publishing, 1999.

Forsyth, Ian K., and Edith M. Rowlings. *A Goodly Heritage*. Dartmouth: Dartmouth Historical Association, 2002.

Gaede, Robert L., and Harold M. Merklinger. *Seas, Ships, and Sensors: An Informal History of the Defence Research Establishment Atlantic, 1968–1995*. Ottawa: Government of Canada, 2003.

Gurney Smith, Marilyn. *The King's Yard*. Halifax: Nimbus Publishing, 1985.

Kitz, Janet. *Shattered City: The Halifax Explosion and the Road to Recovery*. Halifax: Nimbus Publishing, 1989.

———. *Survivors: Children of the Halifax Explosion*. Halifax: Nimbus Publishing, 1992.

MacDonald, A. H. *Mount Hope Then and Now: A History of the Nova Scotia Hospital*. Self published, 1996.

Martin, John P. *The Story of Dartmouth*. Dartmouth: privately printed, 1957.

Martin, John P. *The Moosehead Story in Nova Scotia*. Halifax: Moosehead Breweries, 1965.

Metson, Graham, ed. *The Halifax Explosion: December 6, 1917*. Toronto: McGraw-Hill Ryerson, 1978.

Payzant, Lewis John, and Joan M. Payzant. *Like a Weaver's Shuttle: A History of the Halifax-Dartmouth Ferries*. Halifax: Nimbus Publishing, 1979.

Payzant, Joan M. *Second to None: A History of Public Education in Dartmouth, NS.* Dartmouth: Dartmouth Historical Association, 1993.

Raddall, Thomas. *Halifax: Warden of the North.* Toronto: McClelland and Stewart, 1971.

Ruffman, Alan, and Colin D. Howell, eds. *Ground Zero: A Reassessment of the 1917 Explosion in Halifax Harbour.* Halifax: Nimbus Publishing and the Gorsebrook Research Institute for Atlantic Canada Studies, 1994.

Newspapers

Dartmouth Patriot; Halifax Chronicle; Halifax Daily Echo; Halifax Herald; Halifax Evening Mail; Windsor Tribune

Websites

http://www.envirosoil.com/French-cable-wharf.html
http://www.museum.gov.ns.ca/mma/AtoZ/expships.html
http://www.gov.ns.ca/nsarm/

Archival and private sources

Church records, courtesy of Halifax and Dartmouth churches
Dartmouth Relief Committee Records, Nova Scotia Archives and Records Management
Halifax Relief Commission Records, Nova Scotia Archives and Records Management
Halifax School Board Records, Nova Scotia Archives and Records Management
Letter from Edith (Barss) Baker, December 1917, to her brother overseas
Letter from Harriet (Bishop) Wilson to Robert and Lorna Huestis, January 1969
MacMechan Papers, Nova Scotia Archives and Records Management

IMAGE SOURCES

All the numbers below are page numbers in the text. The letters t and b refer to top and bottom, respectively, and the letters l and r refer to left and right, respectively. C indicates centre. Photos marked with an asterisk (*) are also held at the Maritime Museum of the Atlantic.
Books of views= books of views of the explosion and aftermath were published in 1917 by various publishers, and were repeated in later booklets.

Books of views: 2, 3, 27, 36r, 37b, 38bl, 42b, 44l, 65tl, 65tr, 69, 70t, 73t.

Canadian Hydrographic Service: 83.

Dartmouth Heritage Museum: 9, 104b, 109, 112, 114, 115, 116b, 117tr, 117bl, 118b, 119, 120bl, 121t, 122.

Defence R&D Canada: 90b. (Photo reproduced by permission of Defence R&D Canada—Atlantic.)

Ground Zero (Nimbus Publishing, 1994): 84.

Halifax City Police Archives: 71tl.

Janet F. Kitz Personal Collection: 12, 17, 18, 21, 26, 28, 29t*, 29b, 30tl*, 30tr, 33t, 38t*, 39t*, 39b*, 40l, 45*, 48t, 49b*, 52b, 53t, 54t, 57t, 62b, 63t*, 66t, 67tl, 67b, 68t, 74c, 74b, 77t, 77b, 129.

Maritime Command Museum: 47b, 73b, 74t.

Maritime Museum of the Atlantic: 16b, 72tl, 72tr.

National Archives of Canada: 97t.

Nova Scotia Archives and Records Management: 4, 6–7, 10, 13, 14, 15, 16t, 19, 22, 33b, 36l, 37tl, 41t, 43l, 47t, 48b, 49t, 54b, 56b, 56tl, 58bl, 60c, 61bl, 62t, 68b, 75t, 75b, 76t, 76b, 86, 92t, 92b, 101, 125, 126t, 126b, 127t.

United Memorial Church: 35.

Views of the Disaster in Dartmouth (1917): 87, 88b, 89t, 89b, 90t, 93l, 96t, 96c, 98r, 99t, 103, 104t, 105t, 106t, 113t, 118tl, 120br, 123.

Nellie Adams: 71tr.

Gary Castle: 8, 29c, 30b, 31, 37tr, 38br, 40r, 41b, 42t, 43r, 44r, 46, 50c. 50b, 53b, 56tr, 57c, 57b, 58tl, 58cl, 58c, 59b, 60t, 60b, 61br, 63c, 63b, 64, 65c, 66b, 67tr, 68c, 71c, 71b, 72b, 73c, 130t, 130b, 132b.

William Clarke: 85b.

Dr. G. W. I. Creighton: 51.

James W. Creighton: 107, 108.

Mary Drury: 96b, 97b.

Matthew J. Hughson: 85t, 88t, 93r, 95, 98l, 99c, 99b, 102, 105c, 106c, 110, 111, 113b, 118tr, 120t, 121b, 127b, 131.

Jean Hunter: 52t.

Karel Lesley: 65b.

R. H. Murray: 117tl.

Joan M. Payzant: 79, 100, 105b, 132.

L. J. Payzant: 94, 116t, 117br.

Dorothy Scott: 50t.

Wournell Family: 34.

INDEX

P

Q

R

S

T

U

V

W